A Treatise on *Money*

Sources in Early Modern Economics, Ethics, and Law

General Editors

Jordan J. Ballor, Acton Institute
Stephen J. Grabill, Acton Institute

The disciplines of economics, ethics, and law cannot be detached from a historical background that was; it is increasingly recognized, religious in nature. Economists Adam Smith and Léon Walras drew on the work of sixteenth- and seventeenth-century Spanish theologians who strove to understand the process of exchange and trade in order to better articulate subjective value, a dynamic theory of money, the role of the merchant, and the concept of marginal utility. Likewise, political theorists John Neville Figgis and Otto von Gierke drew on the work of sixteenth- and seventeenth-century Dutch, Swiss, German, and Spanish jurists and ethicists who articulated concepts that laid the foundation for federalist political structures, constitutionalism, popular sovereignty, natural-law jurisprudence, and limited government in the Western legal tradition. After a long period in which economics, ethics, and law became detached from theology, many economists, legal scholars, political theorists, and theologians now see the benefit of studying early modern economic, ethical, and legal texts in their full cultural, often religious, context. This series, *Sources in Early Modern Economics, Ethics, and Law*, provides first-ever English translations and editions of some of the most formative but previously inaccessible texts that shaped the disciplines of economics, ethics, and law in the early modern era and beyond. These inexpensive translations of seminal texts will make substantive contributions to contemporary interdisciplinary discussion.

A Treatise on *Money*

Luis de Molina

Translated by Jeannine Emery

Introduction by Rudolf Schuessler

CLP Academic
Grand Rapids · Michigan
Refo500

A Treatise on Money

Translated by Jeannine Emery

Cover image: Evora panorama
License: Creative Commons Attribution-Share Alike 3.0 Unported
Source: Digitalsignal
URL: http://commons.wikimedia.org/wiki/File:Evora_view.jpg
Inset photo: Wikimedia Commons (http://commons.wikimedia.org/wiki/File:Luis_Molina.jpeg)

ISBN: 978-193894810-7

CHRISTIAN'S LIBRARY PRESS
An imprint of the Acton Institute for the Study of Religion & Liberty
98 E. Fulton
Grand Rapids, Michigan 49503
Phone: 616.454.3080
Fax: 616.454.9454
www.clpress.com

Interior composition by Judy Schafer
Cover design by Peter Ho
Editorial management by Andrew M. McGinnis

Printed in the United States of America

Contents

Series Introduction *ix*

Abbreviations *xxi*

Introduction by Rudolf Schuessler *xxiii*

A Treatise on Money

Argument 396 3

Diverse Senses in Which the Terms *Barter* and *Exchange* May Be Used

To Barter in a Strict Sense

Argument 397 9

Whether the *Alcabala* Should Be Paid in Barter and Exchange Transactions

Argument 398 23

On Exchange in a Strict Sense and Its Types

Is the Exchange Dealer's Activity Licit?

Argument 399 29

Is It Licit for the Exchange Dealer to Receive in the Petty Exchange an Increment over the Price That the Law Has Appraised the Coins For?

Argument 400 37

On Diverse Gold and Silver Coins That Have Been Coined in Castile and Portugal over Time

On Their Value at the Moment of Coinage and at the Present Time

On the Value of Gold and Silver Ingots in These Kingdoms at Different Times

ARGUMENT 401 55

Whether a Higher Price Than the One Set by the Law May Licitly Be Received for the Coins to Which the Public Authority Assigned a Particular Value at the Moment of Coinage

ARGUMENT 402 65

If an Employee Who Was Taking Money in Gold Coins to Pay Some Debts, or to Make Some Purchases, Took Advantage on the Way of an Opportunity Offered to Exchange Those Coins for a Better Price, Could That Employee Appropriate for Himself the Extra Charge Obtained in This Manner?

ARGUMENT 403 71

On the Usefulness of Exchanging Money from One Place to Another

On the Type of Exchange in Which the Banker Receives the Money in Advance

ARGUMENT 404 77

On Whether It Is Licit for the Banker to Charge a Certain Increment for the Exchange He Gives When He Anticipates the Money in One Place to Recover It in a Different Place

ARGUMENT 405 89

Answers to Some Questions Regarding What Has Been Said in the Two Preceding Arguments

What Can Be Said About Those Who for a Salary Bring with Them the Horses They Needed to Rent for the Trip

Is It Licit to Receive an Increment for the Exchange Carried Out from One Place to Another within the Same Kingdom?

ARGUMENT 406 95

On How the Same Amount of Money May Have a Different Value in Different Places

Argument 407 99

If Coins That by Law or Generally Accepted Custom Had a Different Value in Relation to Other Copper Coins of a Lesser Value in Places Also Different, Can They Be Justly Exchanged between Those Places Keeping to the Equality?

Argument 408 107

On the People Who Travel from One Place to Another to Carry Out Exchanges

Argument 409 119

On Some of the Ways in Which Money Is Paid for in the Exchanges

On Bills of Exchange

May the Bankers Licitly Receive Any Other Stipend?

Argument 410 129

On Exchanges and the Different Value of Money in Different Places, Not in Comparison to Small Coins Any Longer but Because of Concurrent Circumstances

Thus, We End Our Study on Money

About the Contributors 143

Sources in Early Modern Economics, Ethics, and Law

Series Introduction

Jordan J. Ballor
Stephen J. Grabill

For the same underlying reasons that moral theology is held in disrepute by many Western intellectuals, modern economists tend to glibly dismiss or even simply ignore the economic ideas of the scholastics, whether those of the twelfth or the seventeenth century. For many intellectuals nowadays, moral theology has come to signify a passé form of religious thinking that embraces irrationality and dogmatism, and economic historians—along with notable astrophysicists, geneticists, paleontologists, political analysts, philosophers, and ethicists—have all espoused this line of thought. Among the latter, in particular, the identification of scholastic economics (or the "canonical concept of market behavior," as it is sometimes called) with Aristotelian metaphysics and ecclesiastical authority has made modern economic professionals reticent or, at the very least unreceptive, to acknowledging any sophisticated analytical contribution to monetary and value theory by the Schoolmen or the Doctors—their sixteenth- and seventeenth-century heirs.

The severing of economic ideas from their original historical and metaphysical contexts becomes especially pronounced in the contemporary debate over the prehistory of economics. Invariably, most mainstream economic historians locate the birth of modern economics in Adam Smith, the mercantilists, and the physiocrats. For historian of economics Mark Blaug, the prehistory of economics begins with the seventeenth-century mercantilists and not, as the revisionists insist, with either the ancient Greeks or the medieval scholastics. He coins the term *pre-Adamite economics* to methodologically define and restrict the era of prehistory to Smith's immediate and direct historical precursors: the seventeenth-century mercantilists, the physiocrats, and the British free-trade writers of the eighteenth century.

The broader question of whether the prehistory of economics should start in the thirteenth century or much earlier is, in Blaug's estimation, "an afterthought."[1] An afterthought, we might infer, which could presumably surface information that would challenge positivist assumptions about human behavior and social cohesion and one that will yield few, if any, new insights into quantitative methods and models. Where the scholastics analyzed economic and commercial transactions as either ethical or legal matters involving the application of natural law to civil contracts, "it was the mercantilists," contends Blaug, "who, long before Adam Smith, broke with the canonical conception of market behavior as a moral problem and fashioned the concept of 'economic man.'" These mercantilists

> believed in the direct power of self-interest and in matters of domestic economic policy came near to advocating laissez-faire. Adam Smith was not the first to have confidence in the workings of the 'invisible hand.' Nor is it necessary to appeal to scholastic influences to account for his grasp of the determination of prices by demand and supply.[2]

1. Mark Blaug, *Economic Theory in Retrospect*, 5th ed. (Cambridge: Cambridge University Press, 1997), 29.

2. Blaug, *Economic Theory in Retrospect*, 31.

Regardless of whether it is necessary to appeal to scholastic influences to explain how Smith, in particular, understood price and value to be determined, such a determination does not speak to the wider issue of whether such seminal figures in the history of economics as Bernardo Davanzati (1529–1606), Hugo Grotius (1583–1645), Samuel von Pufendorf (1632–1694), Gershom Carmichael (1672–1729), Francis Hutcheson (1694–1746), Jean-Jacques Burlamaqui (1694–1748), Adam Ferguson (1723–1816), Ferdinando Galiani (1728–1787), Auguste Walras (1801–1866), and Léon Walras (1834–1910) were influenced by scholastic treatments of price and value. Neither does this judgment determine, for that matter, whether Smith's entire system of thought remains intelligible if the role he assigns to teleology, final causes, divine design, and virtue is disregarded as merely ornamental.[3] In this wider respect, therefore, the modern quibble over scholastic influences in Smith is a red herring because, as Langholm attests, it sidesteps serious historical investigation into the continuities and discontinuities between scholastic and modern economic ideas.[4] Furthermore, it also has the convenient side effect of

3. See James E. Alvey, "The Secret, Natural Theological Foundation of Adam Smith's Work," *Journal of Markets & Morality* 7, no. 2 (Fall 2004): 335–61. See also Paul Oslington, ed., *Adam Smith as Theologian* (New York: Routledge, 2011).

4. "From an analytical and terminological point of view," writes Langholm, "there is much of scholastic teaching that can be seen to have survived into modern economics. This is not surprising, since (at least if this observation is limited to our Western civilization) it was in the high Middle Ages that the foundations were laid for the kind of systematic reasoning about social relationships that has run on continually to the present day. Sometimes, as in the case of the fairness of the market price, it was deemed pertinent above to point out a subtle shift in the moral basis that supported an apparently unaltered doctrine. Elsewhere, where doctrines have changed as radically as in the case of lending at interest, the scholastics can still be credited with posing the terms of an ongoing argument. Therefore, it would seem that much of the old vessel remained to receive new content. The question is how completely it was ever emptied of the

downplaying the importance of teleology and natural theology in the thought of Smith himself and other seventeenth-, eighteenth-, and nineteenth-century political economists.

By methodologically constricting the prehistory of economics to the mercantilists and the physiocrats, as positivist historiographers commend, economic history congeals around such characteristically "modern" concerns as the concept of "economic man," self-interest, and the emancipation of economics from the so-called canonical concept of market behavior. This arbitrary limitation of which ideas and which people carry weight in economic history only serves to bolster twentieth-century positivist assumptions, particularly those of value neutrality and *homo economicus*, the assumption that humans act as rational and self-interested agents who desire wealth, avoid unnecessary labor, and seek to order their decision making exclusively around those goals. In the end, the modern reduction of the prehistory of economics to the seventeenth-century mercantilists can be put in the form of an Occam's razor-like question: Why appeal to scholastic influences to illumine modern notions of money, value, and price when all the basic elements of classical economics are already embedded in mercantilism?

The most straightforward reply is that seminal ideas, which include revolutionary economic ideas, never develop in intel-

---

ferment prepared for it in the medieval schools. This subject requires a book rather than a few lines. In fact, it has been the subject of many books, some of them provoked or inspired by Max Weber's ideas about religion and capitalism. For simplicity, let us recall that scholastic economics rested on three intellectual traditions. The first support was the tradition of the Bible and the Church Fathers with its emphasis on individual duty. The second was the tradition of the recently rediscovered Roman law with its emphasis on individual rights. The two traditions were made to balance briefly and precariously in the Thomist synthesis by means of a third support in Aristotelian social philosophy." See Odd Langholm, "Scholastic Economics," in *Pre-Classical Economic Thought: From the Greeks to the Scottish Enlightenment*, ed. S. Todd Lowry (Boston/Dordrecht/Lancaster: Kluwer Academic Publishers, 1987), 132–33.

lectual, historical, religious, philosophical, or geographical vacuums. "Enlightened," secular reaction to the medieval Church's temporal jurisdiction and to theology's intellectual hegemony as the queen of the sciences has created a modern milieu in which scholars are no longer even aware of the historical influence that fundamental Christian doctrines have exerted in Western culture and university life.[5] From very early times, Christian theologians assumed that the application of patterns of discursive reasoning (as in the scholastic method, which was a method instituted by medieval Christian theologians and adapted and applied for subsequent centuries) could yield an increasingly accurate understanding not only of God's word and moral will but also of the created order itself.

Thus the systematic application of reason to a variety of intellectual undertakings, including economic problems, was not the invention of the Enlightenment. Rather, the application of reason within a coherent intellectual framework is the legacy of Christian scholasticism—the method of the medieval and early modern schools. The application of this scholastic method led to increased understanding of the world and human affairs, and spurred efforts to formulate logical explanations of regular occurrences in nature. "All things possess order amongst themselves: this order is the form that makes the world resemble God," wrote Dante in the *Divine Comedy*.[6] It can be argued that the specific application of scholastic method to economic problems became the seedbed for innovative ideas that, after much dialectical refinement, came to shape the world of modern economics. The truth of this statement does not rest on modernity's own understanding of its birth, development, or future trajectory but rather on the demonstrable "internal interconnec-

5. See Chris L. Firestone and Nathan Jacobs, eds., *The Persistence of the Sacred in Modern Thought* (Notre Dame: University of Notre Dame Press, 2012).

6. Dante, *Paradise*, trans. Anthony Esolen (New York: Modern Library, 2004), 1:103–5, p. 9.

tions and affinities among ideas, their dynamism or 'particular go' (Lovejoy's phrase), and the logical pressures they are capable of exerting on the minds of those that think them."[7]

Assent to this claim, however, will require the positivist historian to reconsider not only the relationship between metaphysical schemata and intellectual traditions, which, in turn, will require an acknowledgement of the indispensable role of theological doctrines in the history of ideas,[8] but it will also require an admission that the recent detachment of economics from morality is itself a novelty, an aberration from a long-standing tradition within political economy itself.[9] In Alvey's judgment,

7. Francis Oakley, *Natural Law, Laws of Nature, Natural Rights: Continuity and Discontinuity in the History of Ideas* (New York and London: Continuum, 2005), 9.

8. See Oakley, *Natural Law, Laws of Nature, Natural Rights*, 13–34. See also the various essays in Oakley's *Politics and Eternity: Studies in the History of Medieval and Early-Modern Political Thought* (Leiden: Brill, 1999); Oakley, *Omnipotence, Covenant, and Order: An Excursion in the History of Ideas from Abelard to Leibniz* (Ithaca: Cornell University Press, 1984); Oakley, *Kingship: The Politics of Enchantment* (Oxford: Blackwell Publishing, 2006); and William J. Courtenay, *Covenant and Causality in Medieval Thought: Studies in Philosophy, Theology, and Economic Practice* (London: Variorum Reprints, 1984).

9. Broadly, on the historical constriction and positivism of contemporary economic thinking, see John D. Mueller, *Redeeming Economics: Rediscovering the Missing Element* (Wilmington, DE: ISI Books, 2010). See also Jeffrey T. Young, *Economics as a Moral Science: The Political Economy of Adam Smith* (Cheltenham, UK: Edward Elgar, 1997); James Alvey, "A Short History of Economics as a Moral Science," *Journal of Markets & Morality* 2, no. 1 (Spring 1999): 53–73; Ricardo F. Crespo, "Is Economics a Moral Science?," *Journal of Markets & Morality* 1, no. 2 (Fall 1998): 201–11; Peter J. Boettke, "Is Economics a Moral Science? A Response to Ricardo F. Crespo," *Journal of Markets & Morality* 1, no. 2 (Fall 1998): 212–19; and Crespo, "Is Economics a Moral Science? A Response to Peter J. Boettke," *Journal of Markets & Morality* 1, no. 2 (Fall 1998): 220–25; Jeffrey T. Young, *Economics as a Moral Science: The Political Economy of Adam Smith* (Cheltenham, UK: Edward Elgar, 1997).

> There are two major reasons why economics has become detached from moral concerns. First, the natural sciences came to be seen as successful, and the attempt was made to emulate that success in economics by applying natural science methods, including mathematics, to economic phenomena. Second, the self-styled economic science came to adopt positivism, which ruled out moral issues from science itself.[10]

It is the latter recognition, perhaps more than any other, that squares the revisionists off against the positivists in the debate over the prehistory of economics.

When the positivistic bias begins to be put aside and we look anew at works from earlier periods, we find the early modern era to be a rich source of intellectual ferment on economic, ethical, and legal and political topics. In the sixteenth and early seventeenth centuries, a small but influential group of theologians and jurists centered in Spain attempted to synthesize the Roman legal texts with Aristotelian and Thomistic moral philosophy. The movement began with the revival of Thomistic philosophy in Paris, where, as Camacho recounts, "Pierre Crockaert underwent an intellectual conversion from nominalist philosophy to the philosophy of Thomas Aquinas."[11]

Shortly before 1225, the year of Aquinas' birth, Aristotle's works on metaphysics, physics, politics, and ethics became available in the West, and, within the span of a generation, Aristotelianism, which had been brought to Europe by Arabic scholars, would be a serious contender in medieval thought. Thomas sought a rapprochement between the Greek philosophical tradition that Aristotle represented and the Christian divine ideas tradi-

10. Alvey, "A Short History of Economics as a Moral Science," 53.

11. Francisco Gómez Camacho, "Later Scholastics: Spanish Economic Thought in the Sixteenth and Seventeenth Centuries," in *Ancient and Medieval Economic Ideas and Concepts of Social Justice*, ed. S. Todd Lowry and Barry Gordon (Leiden and New York: Brill, 1998), 503.

tion articulated by the likes of Augustine, pseudo-Dionysius, and Bonaventure. In 1512, Crockaert published his commentary on the last part of Thomas' *Summa theologicae* with the help of a student, Francisco de Vitoria (ca. 1483–1546).[12]

Approximately two hundred years before Thomas was born, the *Corpus iuris civilis* of Justinian had been rediscovered and had become the object of academic disputation. However, the traditions of Roman law and Aristotelian and Thomistic philosophy existed in relative isolation from one other, at least until the early sixteenth century in Spain. "In the sixteenth and early seventeenth centuries," states Camacho, "a synthesis was finally achieved by that group of theologians and jurists known to historians of law as the 'late scholastics' or the 'Spanish natural law school.'"[13] Schumpeter concurs with this judgment and adds, "It is within their systems of moral theology and law that economics gained definite if not separate existence, and it is they who come nearer than does any other group to having been the 'founders' of scientific economics."[14] The Salamancans in particular, writes Moss,

> were as interested in a general theory of how exchange rates between different currencies are formed as in explaining why a bill of exchange is worth more in one region of Spain

---

12. Camacho, "Later Scholastics: Spanish Economic Thought in the Sixteenth and Seventeenth Centuries," 503.

13. Camacho, "Later Scholastics: Spanish Economic Thought in the Sixteenth and Seventeenth Centuries," 503.

14. Joseph Schumpeter, *History of Economic Analysis*, ed. Elizabeth Booty Schumpeter (Oxford: Oxford University Press, 1954), 97: "And not only that it will appear, even, that the bases they laid for a serviceable and well-integrated body of analytic tools and propositions were sounder than was much subsequent work, in the sense that a considerable part of the economics of the later nineteenth century might have been developed from those bases more quickly and with less trouble than it actually cost to develop it, and that some of that subsequent work was therefore in the nature of a time- and labor-consuming detour."

> than in another region. Was the agio or exchange premium evidence of usury and therefore immoral behavior on the part of merchants and traders, or rather something 'natural' governed by the basic laws of supply and demand?[15]

The case of this so-called School of Salamanca is just one example of the rich intellectual traditions that have far too often been ignored or downplayed by contemporary scholarship. The coherent intellectual framework of Christian scholasticism reverberates not only in the field of economics but also in the related areas of ethics and law. Thus, political theorists John Neville Figgis and Otto von Gierke drew on the work of a variety of sixteenth- and seventeenth-century Dutch, Swiss, German, and Spanish jurists and ethicists who articulated concepts that laid the foundation for federalist political structures, constitutionalism, popular sovereignty, natural-law jurisprudence, and limited government in the Western legal tradition.[16] The diversity and variety of relevant sources from this period is underscored by the contribution of Protestant scholars, who produced significant scholastic works as well as more occasional treatises. Much of the early Protestant thought on economics, ethics, and law attaches to their homiletical and exegetical work in addition to the achievements in systems of moral theology and philosophy. The Dutch Reformed legal thinker Johannes Althusius (1563–1638) stands as a representative example in this regard, and his contributions to the development of Western legal and political traditions

15. Laurence S. Moss, "Introduction," in *Economic Thought in Spain: Selected Essays of Marjorie Grice-Hutchinson*, ed. Laurence S. Moss and Christopher K. Ryan (Brookfield, VT: Edward Elgar, 1993), xv.

16. On Johannes Althusius in particular, see Otto von Gierke, *The Development of Political Theory*, trans. Bernard Freyd (New York: Howard Fertig, 1966), 70; and John Neville Figgis, *Studies of Political Thought: From Gerson to Grotius, 1414–1625* (Cambridge: Cambridge University Press, 1907), 175–85.

are becoming increasingly appreciated.[17] After a long period in which economics, ethics, and law became detached from theology, many economists, legal scholars, political theorists, and theologians now see the benefit of studying early modern economic, ethical, and legal texts in their full cultural, often religious, context.

The Sources in Early Modern Economics, Ethics, and Law series is the latest installment in the excavation of the mines of early modern theological thought on these topics. The aim of this series is to offer economists, intellectual historians, moral theologians, and graduate students in the fields of economics, economic ethics, economic history, banking history, political economy, and moral theology a useful and accessible collection of some of the most important early modern texts in the fields of economics, ethics, and law. Now, for the first time, the unabridged texts of works such as Martín de Azpilcueta's *Commentary on the Resolution of Money* (1556), Luis de Molina's *Treatise on Money* (1597), and Juan de Mariana's *Treatise on the Alteration of Money* (1609), as well as selections from larger works such as Johannes Althusius' *Dicaeologicae* (1617) and Girolamo Zanchi's *Omnium operum theologicorum* (1619) will be available as stand-alone volumes in English translation and in modern editions with scholarly annotations. We hope that the publication of these primary texts in a series of paperbacks will help to facilitate exploration of the continuities and discontinuities, agreements and disagreements, innovations and ruptures among theological communities during the latter half of the sixteenth and the early seventeenth century.

17. See, for instance, John Witte Jr., "A Demonstrative Theory of Natural Law: The Original Contribution of Johannes Althusius," in *Public Theology for a Global Society: Essays in Honor of Max L. Stackhouse*, ed. Deirdre King Hainsworth and Scott R. Paeth (Grand Rapids: Eerdmans, 2010), 21–36; and Thomas O. Hueglin, *Early Modern Concepts for a Late Medieval World: Althusius on Community and Federalism* (Waterloo, ON: Wilfrid Laurier University Press, 1999).

The translations and modern editions (in conjunction with the introductions by leading authorities) will show the sophistication with which Christian thinkers from a variety of confessional and theological perspectives examined issues such as the role and responsibilities of the civil magistrates, the existence and efficacy of natural law, usury, and the ethics of moneylending, as well as the new process of using bills of exchange (*cambium per litteras*) to replace the cumbersome and dangerous transportation of metallic coins between commercial fairs, which led not only to new scholastic insights on interest, credit, and international trade but also to a much more comprehensive analysis of monetary exchange and banking practices than had been undertaken before. The texts will also address the questions as particular as why the same currency was worth more in one region than another area's currency, and, moreover, why the rate of exchange fluctuated between one area and the next. These moral and economic concerns, along with many others, will be addressed in detail throughout the course of the series by some of the leading, and heretofore underappreciated, authorities from the early modern era.

Abbreviations

Cod.	*Corpus Juris Civilis*, Codex.
D.	*Corpus Juris Civilis*, Digesta.
DMA	J. R. Strayer, ed. *Dictionary of the Middle Ages*. 13 vols. New York: Scribner, 1982–1986.
EtR	P. F. Grendler, ed. *Encyclopedia of the Renaissance*. 6 vols. New York: Scribner, 1999.
Inst.	*Corpus Juris Civilis*, Institutiones.
Leis extravagantes	*Leis extravagantes collegidas e relatadas pelo licenciado Duarte Nunez do Liam per mandado do muito alto & muito poderoso rei Dom Sebastiam nosso senhor*. Lisbon: Antonio Gonçaluez, 1569.
NCE	*New Catholic Encyclopedia*. 18 vols. New York: McGraw-Hill, 1967–1989.
N. N. R.	*Novísima Recopilación de las Leyes de España*. 5 vols. Madrid, 1805–1829.
N. R.	*Recopilación delas leyes destos reynos* [or, *Nueva Recopilación*]. Alcala de Henares: Andres de Angulo, 1569.
Ordenações Manuelinas	*Ordenações Manuelinas*. Seville: J. Cronberger, 1521, 1539; Lisbon: G. Gallardo, 1533, 1539; Lisbon: J. Manuel, 1565.

INTRODUCTION

Rudolf Schuessler

The Spaniard Luis de Molina (1535–1600) was one of the most eminent theologians of the Jesuit order in the sixteenth century.[1] From 1551 to 1562, Molina studied law in Salamanca; philosophy in Alcalá de Henares (both in Spain); and theology in Coimbra, Portugal. Having joined the Jesuits in 1553, he taught theology after 1563 in Coimbra, Évora, Cuenca, and finally Madrid. Molina's fame rests mainly on his work in two subjects. He developed a groundbreaking theory of human freedom of action against Protestant and Catholic defenders of a far-reaching predetermination of human agency. His theory sparked a new branch of liberty-oriented Catholic thought, called Molinism, and exerted a considerable influence on the emerging modern discourse on human freedom.[2] Molina's other major contribution to early

1. On Molina in general, see Matthias Kaufmann and Alexander Aichele, eds., *A Companion to Luis de Molina* (Leiden: Brill, 2014).

2. For Molina on liberty, see Alexander Aichele, "The Real Possibility of Freedom," in *A Companion to Luis de Molina*, 3–54; Marcelino Ocaña García, *Molinismo y libertad* (Córdoba: Publicaciones Obra Social y Cultural Cajasur, 2000).

modern thought was in the field of economics and contract law, about which he wrote a monumental treatise, *On Justice and Right* (*De iustitia et iure*), from which the present translation of the section on money and exchange (*De cambiis*) is taken.[3]

Our author's economic thought is less novel and daring than his theory of freedom. His most prominent theses on money and exchange had already emerged in the first half of the sixteenth century, when a revival of scholastic thought (that is, the medieval form of academic thought) engendered a wealth of new ideas.[4] New economic ideas were cultivated in Paris, Rome, Tübingen, and Salamanca. In Salamanca, professors Juan de Medina (1490–1547) and Martín de Azpilcueta (1491–1586) discovered an explanation for price inflation that is still valid, and established a relation between the quantity of money supply,

3. Molina's *De iustitia et iure* first appeared in press in 1593 (Cuenca). Here, the easily web-accessible (www.bsb-muenchen.de) six-volume edition of 1659 (Mainz) is used for reference. Manuel Fraga Iribarne edited the work in Spanish in 1941–44, and some partial recent editions exist: Luis de Molina, *La teoría de justo precio*, ed. Francisco Gómez Camacho (Madrid: Editora Nacional, 1981); Luis de Molina, *Tratado sobre los cambios*, ed. Francisco Gómez Camacho (Madrid: Instituto de Cooperacion Iberoamericana, 1990).

4. On early modern (Spanish) scholastic economic thought, see in general José Barrientos Garcia, *Un siglo de moral económia en Salamanca, 1526–1629* (Salamanca: Ediciones Universidad de Salamanca, 1985); Alejandro Chafuen, *Faith and Liberty* (Lanham, MD: Lexington, 2003); Abelardo del Vigo Gutiérrez, *Economía y ética en el siglo XVI* (Madrid: Biblioteca de Autores Cristianos, 2006); Francisco Gómez Camacho, *Economía y filosofía moral. La formación del pensamiento económico europeo en la Escolástica española* (Madrid: Síntesis, 1998); Marjorie Grice-Hutchinson, *The School of Salamanca: Readings in Spanish Monetary Theory, 1544–1605* (Oxford: Clarendon, 1952). On Molina's economic thought, see Diego Alonso-Lasheras, *Luis de Molina's* De Iustitia et Iure (Leiden: Brill, 2011); Rudolf Schuessler, "The Economic Thought of Luis de Molina," in *A Companion to Luis de Molina*, 257–88; Wilhelm Weber, *Wirtschaftsethik am Vorabend des Liberalismus. Höhepunkt und Abschluß der scholastischen Wirtschaftsbetrachtung durch Ludwig Molina S. J. (1535–1600)* (Münster: Aschendorff, 1959).

demand for money, and inflation. Molina discusses these relations in argument 401 and following, adding detail and lucidity to an emerging theory. He was the first Jesuit to analyze economic issues at length and in a full-scale treatise (*On Justice and Right*), thus setting the pace for important successors in his order, such as Leonard Lessius (1554–1623) and Juan de Lugo (1583–1660).[5] Jesuit economic thought in the seventeenth century gravitated toward individual freedom and displayed a keen appreciation of the market economy while upholding moral restrictions for market activities in a flexible and low-profile form. These features of Jesuit economic thought are of great—although not universally recognized—importance because the Jesuits were the teaching order par excellence in early modernity. Almost all early modern economic thinkers in Catholic countries were taught by the Jesuits, and Molina had the privilege to set the agenda for his order's economic thought.

From a present-day perspective, using the phrase *economic thought* with respect to Molina and his scholastic colleagues may appear to be an overstatement. Modern economics is mathematical, but even if we bracket this rather recent development, it is also positive, that is, concerned with the causes and effects of economic activities. The moral evaluation of economic activities, which was the main focus of medieval theologians, is not a core issue of modern economics. In a not always peaceful cohabitation with medieval jurists, theologians discussed the moral legitimacy or sinfulness of economic contracts. They often noted expert disagreement concerning these issues, recognizing that contracts had to be approved or rejected under moral uncertainty about

5. The first treatise entitled *De Iustitia et Iure* was by the Dominican scholar Domingo de Soto: *De iustitia et iure libri decem* (Lyon, 1559). The Jesuit tradition of such treatises continued notably with Leonard Lessius, *De iustitia et iure ceterisque virtutibus* (Venetiis, 1617) and Juan de Lugo, *Disputationes de iustitia et iure* (Lyon, 1646). On the interplay between morality and contract law exemplified by these treatises, see Wim Decock, *Theologians and Contract Law* (Leiden: Martinus Nijhoff, 2013).

their legitimacy. Differentiated rules for decision making under (moral) uncertainty helped to solve these problems.[6] In sum, a moral-theological perspective prevailed in medieval economics, and it has characterized Catholic economic thought up to the present day. In the sixteenth century, however, the first steps were taken toward analyzing the causes and effects of economic activities without immediate recourse to questions of sin and sin avoidance. Molina is an exponent of this trend. We may therefore date the beginnings of a systematic positive analysis of markets and their functioning to the sixteenth century. This is not to denigrate the importance of Adam Smith, but only a reminder that significant steps on the way to Smithian economics were taken long before Smith. Although the positive economic analyses in question unfold under the umbrella of a moral framework, they nevertheless resemble an early form of economic thought as we know it.

For related reasons, Molina has been styled as a precursor of modern liberalism.[7] His championing of individual freedom in the spheres of metaphysics, economics, and morality (although not, of course, in the sphere of religion) informs continental, and often Catholic, versions of liberal thought. Naturally, the morally circumscribed claims of a late-scholastic author are not characteristic of Anglo-American brands of liberalism, but we should remember that the Anglo-American tradition does

6. Moral decision making under uncertainty was developed with many applications to economic problems in early modern casuistry and probabilism. Studies of scholastic economic thought often fail to reflect the importance of this background. For a short analysis of probabilism with respect to Molina's thought, see Schuessler, "Economic Thought of Luis de Molina," 286.

7. Molina's "liberalism" is discussed in Chafuen, *Faith and Liberty*, chap. 12; Peter Chojnowski, "'Corporation Christendom': The True School of Salamanca," *The Angelus* 28, no. 1 (January 2005): 8–20, http://www.angelusonline.org/uploads/articles_issue_pdf/1_2005_jan.pdf; Gómez Camacho, *Economía*, 283; Murray Rothbard, *Economic Thought before Adam Smith* (Cheltenham, UK: Edward Elgar, 1996), 113; Weber, *Wirtschaftsethik*.

not encompass the entirety of modern forms of liberalism. European social economies (such as the German form) are often heavily influenced by Catholic forms of liberalism and, in the final analysis, by thinkers like Molina, whose thought marks the liberal end of the spectrum in his generation.

Money and Quantity Theory

In argument 406, Molina plainly states: "In equal circumstances, the more abundant money is in one place, so much less is its value to buy things or to acquire things that are not money."[8] Thus he documents some understanding of the ceteris-paribus character of economic laws, as well as of the relationship between supply and demand on markets. As money supply increases, the rate of exchange between money and other goods decreases, and the prices of the goods in question rise. Molina, however, was not the first to postulate this relationship. Juan de Medina had already recognized in 1546 that the value of money varies with its abundance and scarcity, and with the number of buyers and sellers.[9] By the 1570s, Martín de Azpilcueta, Jean Bodin, and Tomás de Mercado had published similar observations, establishing the first tenets of what came to be called the quantity theory of money.[10] According to the quantity theory, the price level of goods is proportional to money supply. As does Azpilcueta, Molina observes that the price for gold, or in general the value of money, is lower in South America than in Spain, and in Spain lower than in other European countries (arg. 406).

---

8. See page 96 below.

9. Juan de Medina, *De poenitentia, restitutione, et contractibus* (1st ed., 1546; 1581; repr., Farnborough, UK: Gregg, 1967), 312.

10. The origins of the quantity theory are discussed in Abelardo del Vigo Gutiérrez, *Cambistas, mercaderes y banqueros* (Madrid: Biblioteca de Autores Cristianos, 1997), 22; Gómez Camacho, *Economía*, chap. 6; José Larraz, *La época del mercantilismo en Castilla, 1500–1700*, 3rd ed. (Madrid: Aguilar, 1963), chap. 3.

In fact, Europe underwent a prolonged period of price inflation in the sixteenth century. Hence, the influx of precious metals from South America and the inflation it caused in Europe seems to have fostered economic considerations that led to the quantity theory of money. This is at least a good story, and probably one containing a grain of truth. It is not clear, however, whether the price inflation of the sixteenth century was primarily caused by Inca gold and silver or other probable causes. Early modern warfare, for instance, became excessively expensive, and Spain's ruler, Emperor Charles V, was almost constantly at war. Charles V incurred huge debts for financing wars and other imperial policies. The resulting European credit bubble may have stimulated price inflation no less than American specie did.[11]

American specie began to flow into Spain in quantity only from the second half of the sixteenth century onward, but the law of supply and demand was already basically understood in the Middle Ages. Medieval economic thinkers knew how the abundance and scarcity of a good, and the availability of buyers and sellers, influence the direction of prices. Yet they stuck to the Aristotelian doctrine of money as a yardstick of value and a medium of exchange. Hence, they did not regard money as a good that functioned in the same way as other goods. Official restrictions to trading money in the same way as other goods buttressed this view. In the sixteenth century, however, money was increasingly treated as an ordinary good. Molina's discussion of the government's practice of exchange rate fixing for gold and silver coins is a good example of this process (see arg. 401 and following). Although he accepts the regulations, he interprets them in a general framework of principles of justice. In Molina's time, it became generally acknowledged that money is a commodity

11. For a fascinating account of how early modern banks managed to handle this credit bubble (and its occasional bursting), see Mauricio Drelichman and Hans-Joachim Voth, *Lending to the Borrower from Hell: Debt, Taxes, and Default in the Age of Philip II* (Princeton: Princeton University Press, 2014).

(*pecunia est merx*). Given this insight, the quantity theory follows from long-held assumptions concerning supply and demand.

Molina and his colleagues discussed supply and demand effects on a broad scale. Reflecting on the need for money as a market factor (arg. 406), Molina mentions court expenditure and war expenses—two factors that may have been crucial for price inflation in early modern Europe. He is also aware of the variability of prices in different markets and over time, noting systematic price differences between the beginning, middle, and end of a fair due to variations in the number of visitors. Factors of price determination also vary geographically, which leads to price differences and different valuations of currencies in distant markets. Money changers (*campsores*) and bankers have the important task of alleviating the scarcity of money and credit in distant markets (see arg. 408). They should therefore be praised, and they should not be accused of usury unless there are solid reasons to do so. In fact, the contribution of money changers and merchants to the well-functioning of markets, and hence to the common good, was hardly ever more obvious than in the sixteenth century, when human economies truly became global for the first time.[12] Spanish silver from Peru traveled west via Manila to China, paying for commodities transported around Africa to Renaissance Europe, and from there goods were delivered to colonial Peru, forming a circle of commodities and money that literally spanned the globe. Nobody was more keenly aware of this "first globalization" than the Jesuits, Molina's order. At the time of the writing of Molina's *On Justice and Right*, the Jesuits launched their centuries-long engagement with the imperial court of China. The Jesuits, the most globalized of all Catholic orders, understood that neither their mission nor the

12. Molina's global perspective on trade is well expressed in *De iustitia et iure*, tract. 2, disp. 408, and Gómez Camacho, introduction to *Tratado sobre los cambios*, xxvii.

global aspirations of the Spanish crown were sustainable without global trade in money and commodities.

Usury

One impediment for integrated money markets was the long-standing prohibition of usury. *Usury* was a technical term in medieval jurisprudence and theology, referring to the taking of interest on loans (and loans only).[13] Actually, the usury prohibition mainly pertained to interest rates fixed by express agreement as a precondition of a loan. A "voluntary" payment of interest at varying bank-determined rates, which medieval banks offered for deposits to attract depositors, was not universally considered as usurious. During the Middle Ages, further exceptions from the usury prohibition accumulated, and it is an issue for debate how much the remaining loop-holed prohibition impeded medieval economies. The old deregulatory narrative of classical economics clearly needs critical reconsideration. The ban on fixed-interest loans, which was handled as flexible in the later Middle Ages, may well have stimulated the formation of risk capital (there was no prohibition on gains from economic risk-taking) that proved indispensable for the global expansion of European economies. Molina's analysis of usury came at the end of a long process of mitigating and adapting normative restrictions to an ever more expansive and global market economy. Of course, early modern Catholic moral theology never lifted the ban on usury. Yet Molina (in arg. 318 and 356, which are not in the present translation) and his contemporaries took probably the last important mitigating step in the anti-usury tradition by acknowledging risk of

13. On scholastic treatments of usury, see Odd Langholm, *Economics in the Medieval Schools: Wealth, Exchange, Value, Money, and Usury according to the Paris Theological Tradition, 1200–1350* (Leiden: Brill, 1992); John T. Noonan, *The Scholastic Analysis of Usury* (Cambridge, MA: Harvard University Press, 1957); for Molina, see Alonso-Lasheras, *Molina's* De Iustitia et Iure, 126–47; Schuessler, "Economic Thought of Luis de Molina," 276–82.

capital (*periculum sortis*) as a justification for interest.[14] That is, a lender is entitled to demand interest on a loan as compensation for risking the loss of his or her capital, whenever a reasonable fear of non-repayment might exist. Although there were limits on what constituted reasonable fear, this entitlement virtually legitimized interest for loans on a broad scale.

In arguments 408–410, Molina touches on questions of usury in money exchange. Demanding interest or fees for a transaction was considered licit if interpretable as price for the activities of the money changer, or for risk-taking. In this respect, geographical distance between the markets in which a transaction occurred served as an indicator for the legitimacy of interest or fees. Molina also considered liquidity preference as legitimate. Economic agents were entitled to prefer cash now to a legally and nominally equivalent future payment. What never became accepted in scholastic thought was pure time preference. The fact that most people prefer present cash to future cash had no legitimate normative import for Molina and other scholastic economic thinkers. Classical economists, in contrast, had no compunction to let others pay for one's own time preference, but today pure time preference is again hotly disputed in contexts of ecological sustainability or justice for future generations.[15]

Conclusion

Luis de Molina's economic and monetary thought is Janus-faced. It looks back to the ideas of medieval precursors and forward to innovations, which came into their own in modern economics. By summarizing and discussing the state of the art of his time, Molina sets the pace for Jesuit economic thought. After the demise of the scholastic tradition and the temporary abolition of

14. See Alonso-Lasheras, *Molina's* De Iustitia et Iure, 146; Noonan, *Usury*, chap. 14.

15. See Axel Gosseries and Lukas H. Meyer, eds., *Intergenerational Justice* (Oxford: Oxford University Press, 2009).

the Jesuit order in the eighteenth century, the respective doctrines traveled on back roads into the nineteenth century where they influenced the Austrian school and the marginalist revolution in economics.[16] Molina and his contemporaries were the first to apply the laws of supply and demand systematically to money markets, and as a result conceived the quantity theory of inflation. They began to understand the role of risk, of liquidity, and of time preference in economic contexts, as well as the institutional role of property rights. For this they still deserve our attention.

16. See the remarks in Odd Langholm, *Price and Value in the Aristotelian Tradition* (Oslo: Universitetsforlaget, 1979), 140.

A Treatise on *Money*

Argument 396*

Diverse Senses in Which the Terms *Barter* and *Exchange* May Be Used

To Barter in a Strict Sense

Assuming that to barter or truck is similar to exchanging, and both are similar to the purchase and sale operation,[1] it is neces-

* Ed. note: Luis de Molina's *A Treatise on Money* (arguments 396–410) was originally published as part of a collection of consecutively arranged arguments on contracts in volume 2 of his multivolume work, *De iustitia et iure* (Cuenca, 1597). The full collection of these arguments on contracts, including the ones preceding 396 and following 410, can be found in Ludovico Molina, *De iustitia et iure, tomus secundus de contractibus* (Mainz, 1602). Molina makes numerous references to earlier and later arguments in the pages to follow. Readers interested in reviewing those arguments should consult volume two of *De iustitia et iure*. The present translation of arguments 396–410 was based on the modern Spanish translation, *Tratado sobre los cambios*, edición, introducción, y notas por Francisco Gómez Camacho, in the series *Clásicos del Pensamiento Económico Español* (Madrid: Instituto de Estudios Fiscales, 1990). An earlier version of this translation was first published in *Journal of Markets & Morality* 8, no. 1 (2005): 199–323, and subsequently in Stephen J. Grabill, ed., *Sourcebook in Late-Scholastic Monetary Theory* (Lanham, MD: Lexington, 2007), 139–238. Except where indicated by "Ed. note," all notes are original to the author, although the author's notes have been updated to reflect modern citation conventions.

1. D. 19.4.2.

sary to explain them. To exchange means the same as to barter, since, in a wider sense both terms mean the same.[2] However, both terms are used in a triple sense.

First, in a very broad sense, they mean any type of exchange or commutation and, in this sense, they apply to any nongratuitous contract, such as the buying, the renting, the *mutuo*,[3] and all other nongratuitous contracts, both those specifically provided for by the law (nominate) as well as those that are not (innominate).[4] They are all called nongratuitous because in all of them something is done, promised, or given as payment for something received. This was the first sense in which they used the term *barter* or *exchange*, and all the other meanings were acquired as a result of use and have a narrower scope. This explains why they are not called contracts that are specifically provided for by the law (nominate), because in order for a contract to be judged as specifically provided for by the law it should not only keep its generic name due to custom but also be named as a result of its own particularities.[5] Because we are only dealing here with specific contracts, this is not the right time to take on the exchange and barter in such a broad sense.

The second meaning has a narrower scope and refers to the innominate contract expressed in the phrase *do ut des*, that is, one thing is exchanged for a different one, both if the first is considered indeterminate as individual, but specifically or generically

2. Diego de Covarrubias y Leyva, *De collatione veterum nummismatum* (Venice, 1581), c. 7, no. 5. Ed. note: Cf. Covarrubias, *Opera omnia* (Venice, 1581), t. 1.

3. Ed. note: *mutuo*: actual contract in which money, oil, grain, or any other fungible thing is given, so that the other party takes it as one's own, with the obligation to restore the same quantity and the same kind on a designated date.

4. Ed. note: Innominate contracts are those that lack any special nomination or classification in the law.

5. See argument 253.

distinct, as if both are considered individually determinate.[6] This contract is called one of barter or exchange because of use or custom but is different from the rest of the contracts, both the nominate and the innominate. And it applies to the two parts that constitute it: one, that by which one good not considered to be price is exchanged for another not considered to be price either, as when a horse is exchanged for an ox, wheat for oil, one horse for another, and so forth. The other part, that by which a good considered price is exchanged for another also considered price, as when we exchange gold coins for others that are silver, or coins from one place for coins from another. Because the contract in which something not considered price is exchanged for another considered such is a contract, we call it a contract of sale, and thus, nominate.

Because of what we have said about barter and exchange as an innominate contract, in this second sense of the term all contracts specifically provided for by the law (nominate) are excluded, such as the buying, the renting one, and so forth. Because of what we have added to indicate that it is a contract in which a good is exchanged (not something that is done or a service) for another good, the other three innominate contracts are also excluded, that is, those known as *do ut facias*, *facio ut des*, and *facio ut facias*, in which at least one of the parties is exchanging something that is done or a service. Here we intend to discuss bartering in this second sense and its parts; and it shall not be necessary to add other particular arguments about the other innominate contracts, as they do not present any special difficulty and may be sufficiently understood with what has already been expounded in argument 253 and with what we shall say on bartering and the rest of the contracts.

---

6. See argument 253, where Ignacio de Lassarte quotes Padilla, Pinel, and others with whom he agrees. Ignacio de Lassarte, *De decima venditionis et permutationis* (Madrid, 1599), c. 17, no. 7.

The third sense in which the terms *barter* and *exchange* are used is even more precise. To barter means the exchange in which none of the things being bartered is considered as price, for example, a horse for an ox. Exchange is the contract where both of the things being exchanged are considered as price and, in this sense, the exchange is different from the barter. It is in this sense that we shall study the exchange.

To barter or truck, in this third sense, is much like the buying and selling, because of which we may apply to it anything we say about this last contract, as long as the laws do not say differently.[7] For this same reason, in the barter or truck contract, and in the cases in which they could be applied to the contract of sale, there may be loss of rights, redhibitory action, and the *quantominoris*.[8] Things may also be bartered when they have not come into existence but in hopes of when they do, because they can also be bought and sold like this, as proved in argument 340, and as long as there is nothing against it.[9] The same may be said of exchanging in a strict sense. Moreover, when buying and selling of a certain good is forbidden, then it is fair to conclude that its barter is also forbidden.

It is uncertain whether property rights are transferred in the barter and exchange as in the buying and selling operation, that is, not when the good is delivered but when the price or corresponding fee has been paid or is considered paid, as said in argument 338. Some laws[10] determine that such a way of transferring property rights pertains solely to the contract of sale, because of special privilege, and that in the barter as in all

7. D. 19.4.2; Cod. 4.64.2; argument 253.

8. Ed. note: *quanti minoris* is the action of reducing the price for defects in an article sold.

9. Martín de Azpilcueta, *Manual de confesores y penitentes* (Salamanca, 1556), cap. 17, no. 287. Contra Domingo de Soto, *De iustitia et iure, libri decem* (Salamanca, 1553) and Silvestre de Prierias, *Sylvestrina summa, qua summa summarum merito nuncupatur* (Lyons, 1555).

10. Cod. 4.64.2; D. 19.4.1; Cod. 2.3.20.

other contracts in which property rights are transferred, the transference is carried out before the other party complies with the contractual obligations, which the law seems to agree with;[11] although Bartolus and the gloss judge differently,[12] that is, that in the barter and in all other contracts the property rights are not transferred by merely delivering the good, but the other party is required to meet the terms of the contract.[13] I think, however, that the first opinion is better, which seems much more in accordance with the two paragraphs from the *Institutiones* cited earlier. In addition, the fact that in the barter the property rights are transferred before the other party complies with the contract is so clear in the law[14] that it is surprising that Bartolus does not take this law into account, nor does the law that he refers to in order to prove his argument demonstrate anything at all, not even in appearance. For it only says that if the debtor goes to his creditor to ask for the security that he left as guarantee saying he wants to pay the debt, and then later the debtor spends the collateral with whom he had previously decided upon in order not to pay the debt, the creditor shall withhold his right over the security that was fraudulently taken away from him for the period of time it takes to pay the debt. I cannot see how Bartolus may conclude anything from this that would prove his argument.

On the barter or truck, in this third sense, it should be noted that the Portuguese ordinances,[15] in order to avoid the evils that follow, forbid the barter of wheat, wine, oil, or any other kind of good resulting from the year's crop for another good that

11. Inst. 2.1.1.41.

12. Cod. 4.64.2; D. 13.7.3.

13. D. 13.7.3.

14. Cod. 4.64.4.

15. *Ordenações Manuelinas*, lib. 2, tit. últ. Ed. note: The *Ordenações Manuelinas* was the most important compilation of Portugese law in the sixteenth century. It was first published in 1512 and revised and published in a new authoritative edition in 1521. This version, which itself went through several editions, remained in force until 1603.

is to be paid in the future. It also forbids that the person with whom the barter is carried out should buy from someone else. And on those who barter in this way a penalty of *ipso facto* loss of the bartered good is imposed, and that good shall be given to the other person, who shall not have the obligation to repay in any way, nor shall he be able to waive the privilege that the law grants him.

The benefits of bartering or trucking shall be commented upon when we discuss them.

ARGUMENT 397

WHETHER THE *ALCABALA*[*] SHOULD BE PAID IN BARTER AND EXCHANGE TRANSACTIONS

According to Castilian law, not only should the *alcabala* be paid when bartering, but it should be paid twice over: one for each of the goods that are bartered. As a matter of fact, each barter operation is considered to be a double sale transaction:[1] one for each of the individuals participating in the barter. For this reason, in Castile, each of the two are required to pay the *alcabala* according to the value of the good they receive in exchange for the one that was given, because each receives it as if it were its price, and, as we all know, in Castile the seller is required to pay the total amount of the *alcabala* according to the good's price.[2]

---

* Ed. note: *alcabala*: a tribute of a certain percentage of the price paid to the tax authorities by the seller in the contract of sale and by both contracting parties in the contract of barter.

1. D. 21.1.63.

2. N. R. 9.17.2. Ed. note: The *Nueva Recopilación* (i.e., *Recopilación delas leyes destos reynos*) was the principal Spanish law code of 1569. Prior to 1569 the Catholic Kings Ferdinand and Isabella assigned the title *Ordinamentum* to the collected *novellae*, that is, authoritative determinations (such as laws, edicts, judgments, and so forth) that had been compiled into various legal digests (*DMA*, 7:429–30, s.v. "Law Codes: 1000–1500"; and *DMA*, 7:522–23, s.v. "Law, Spanish").

In Portugal the same requirement to pay the tax exists and, for the same reason already mentioned, it is paid by the two individuals who participate in the transaction. Over there it is called *sisa*, as *da sisa* appears in articles. However, each individual pays only half of the tax, because in Portugal, the seller pays half the tax and the buyer the other half, as mentioned when dealing with the buying and selling operation.[3]

There is one point of uncertainty regarding this issue. Because bartering is not considered perfect or complete before the good has been delivered by both parties, nor is it enough that only one of the parties deliver it, as pointed out in argument 253 and as Lassarte acknowledges,[4] it is uncertain if the tax or taxes start to be owed only when the bartering has been completely finished, so that they should not be paid if only one of the individuals delivered the good or if, as pointed out in argument 258, once the delivery is carried out by only one of the parties, it is this party who should pay the tax. Finally, it is uncertain whether there is an obligation to pay the *alcabala* if the individuals decide to rescind the contract before carrying out the delivery.

According to common law, effective in Portugal as nothing has been legislated contradicting it, Lassarte[5] and Bartachino Firmio acknowledge that the tax is not due until the barter is concluded by both parties. According to Menchaca[6] the same happens in Castile, because even if here the right for judicial action is granted for the mere barter pact, then it is not licit to change one's mind either when one of the parties has carried

3. See Ignacio de Lassarte, *De decima venditionis et permutationis* (Madrid, 1599), in schollis ad leg. 2. cit., ante c. 1 and 17, no. 1.

4. Lassarte, *De decima venditionis et permutationis*, c. 17, no. 3; D. 19.4.1.

5. Lassarte, *De decima venditionis et permutationis*, no. 25; Barachino Firmio, *Tractatus de gabellis* (Lyons, 1533), part. 3, partis 8, no. 48.

6. F. Vázquez de Menchaca, *Controversiarum usu frequentium libri tres* (Barcelona, 1563), lib. 1, c. 11, no. 11; Lassarte, *De decima venditionis et permutationis*, c. 17, no. 35.

out the delivery, or even if neither has carried it out;[7] however, the pact or accord to carry out and complete the barter is one thing and the action of bartering itself is a different one, which is neither considered complete nor finished before the two intervening parties carry out the delivery of their respective good. In this kingdom of Castile, the second law mentioned before does not levy the *alcabala* on the barter pact but on the barter itself.

Lassarte has the contrary opinion in the already cited number 25 and says that in Castile this tax is paid once the barter pact has been fulfilled, even if the delivery is never carried out and the individuals rescind the contract by mutual agreement before the delivery is fulfilled. He holds this opinion on account of the fact that because in this kingdom a mere civil pact is enough to establish the obligation between the individuals, and an action may be brought by any one of them, and one may not withdraw against the other one's wishes if one or both of the parties failed to fulfill the delivery, it follows that, in this kingdom, the barter is also perfect and complete by the mere consent of both parties, as happens with the buy-sell contract. Thus, just as in the buying and selling operation, the mere consent is enough for the tax officials to have the right to collect the tax, without being able to defend oneself by bringing into play the contract's rescission by the parties' mutual consent and before carrying out the delivery, so it is with bartering, and the tax must be paid to the one who is recipient and collector of it at the time of the parties' agreement, and not to the one who may exist at the time of delivery. If the above were not true, once the contract had been executed by mutual agreement and in order to evade taxes, the contracting parties would be able to delay its fulfillment and the delivery of the goods while they allowed it, and meanwhile the door would be open to the rescission of the contract if the circumstances were favorable to it.

7. See arguments 257 and 258.

However, there are better grounds for the opposing argument, which many doctors defend and which is based on what we all know, which is that to barter does not refer to the barter pact but to the business of bartering itself, which is only considered complete and finished once the mutual delivery of the goods has been carried out, just as *mutuum*[8] is not understood as a pact or agreement to lend but as the real business of lending itself. And just as the *mutuum* belongs to the contracts specifically provided for by the law (nominate) that perfect themselves with the deed, not only with the consent or with words as seen in argument 254, so bartering belongs to the kind of contract that perfects itself with the deed carried out, since this is what the term *bartering* means, and not the mere consent nor agreement between the parties to barter something.[9]

Therefore, as long as the tax we referred to is levied on bartering, it follows that neither is such tax due, nor do the tax authorities have the right to collect it before the barter is fulfilled. And it does not make any difference if the individuals performing the barter decide among themselves to delay it in order to cancel out the pact if it so suits them, as they would be exercising their full rights and in no way failing in their duty to the tax authorities.

Observe that exactly as according to common law an action may not be brought against the other party if there was only an agreement to carry out a *mutuum*, it may be brought against him if said pact were coupled to another contract, precisely as was said in argument 253. Likewise, according to common law, or in the kingdom of Portugal where only this law is applied in this matter and the tax is levied on the barter, if there were an agreement to barter certain goods or the barter agreement were associated to another contract, the right to bring an action that originates

8. Ed. note: *mutuum*: a type of loan agreement by which a lender lends money or things upon agreement that the borrower will return an equal number, type, and quality of such things at the end of the contract, with or without interest.

9. D. 19.4.1.

in such an agreement shall be acknowledged. However, because the barter has not been carried out thus far and there has only been an agreement, although concealed under the principle of stipulation or association to another contract, the tax shall not affect this agreement, as it only affects the barter contract, or the contract of sale. This explains why, according to the law in use in this kingdom, it becomes unacceptable that for the mere agreement to barter (the same as for any other agreement) the right to bring an action should be granted and the parties be denied the right to revoke the agreement, stating that because of said agreement they owe the tax that is levied on barter contracts.

The reason why the tax is due in the contract of sale and the tax authorities hold the right to collect it for the mere fact of the parties having reached an agreement is very different. As set forth in argument 254 and explained in several others, the buying and selling operation is considered complete and perfect with the individuals' consent, and the term *buy-sell* refers to the already finished and completed contract, because of which it is sufficient for a person to owe the tax levied on it.

This explanation shall make it easy to understand that if in Castile or in Portugal an agreement is reached to barter some particular goods in times of a specific tax collector, but the barter is completed through the delivery of said goods in times of a different tax collector, it is this last tax collector to whom the tax belongs, as it was during the time when he was tax collector that the barter was completed. This would happen even if the initial agreement between the parties were concealed under the guise of mere stipulation and association with a different agreement. This is so because the tax is due not for the barter agreement, even if the civil obligation to fulfill it is originated in this agreement, but for the barter itself once it has been fulfilled, and it was fulfilled not in times of the first tax collector but in times of the second one.

Lassarte[10] believes that the tax levied on the barter is due because the civil obligation is already originated in the pact by which the parties commit themselves to barter. He raises the question of whether the tax should be paid to the first tax collector or to the second one when the barter pact—which the common law says does not give origin to the civil obligation unless it is tied together to another contract or was stipulated by the parties—is carried out during one tax collector's period and the delivery carried out during another's period when the civil obligation starts to be in force. He mentions the opinion of Antonio Gómez,[11] with whom Parladorius agrees and who states that it is the first tax collector who is due the tax. They believe this because, according to them, such obligation does not derive from the fulfillment of the pact and the delivery of the good, but from the pact itself that is followed by the delivery, this being only a condition that makes the obligation not derive from the pact alone.[12] From which follows *sensu contrario*, that if the pact and the contract are followed by something else then there will be a right to take the legal action that is deemed convenient. And they say that since the pact that gives origin to that action was carried out during the first tax collector's period, it follows that it is to him that the tax should be paid, even if the conditions necessary to give origin to that right take place during the second one's period.[13]

I consider Lassarte's opinion much better, that is, that the tax is due to the second tax collector and not to the first. In the first place, because the civil obligation is originated in both parts, and they are both essential to the contract and necessary for it to be

10. Lassarte, *De decima venditionis et permutationis*, c. 17, no. 43.

11. Antonio Gómez, *Opus praeclarum et utilissimum super legibus Tauri* (Salamanca, 1567), c. 8, no. 2; Parladorius, *De rerum quotidianarum libri duo* (Salamanca, 1595), c. 3 § 3, no. 35.

12. Cod. 4.64.3.

13. The gloss of the *leg. Placito* (Cod. 4.64.3), and the Inst. *de actionib. verb. ex permutatione* seem to agree with this opinion.

considered complete and for the obligation to derive from it, as the law says.[14] And if there is anything *a sensu contrario* that the words that cite the *ex placito* law[15] prove, it is merely that the obligation derives from the pact only in a particular way, which we do not deny, but they do not prove that at the same time the obligation does not derive from the delivery itself as part and an addition to the same contract. In the second place, because even if we say it derives only from the pact, once the condition of delivery is fulfilled, it cannot be denied that in order for the contract to be complete and fulfilled, the delivery should take place, which happens during the period of the second tax collector and, in consequence, to him should the tax be paid. The same happens when a contract of sale is held up until the deed is written—it is not considered complete and finished and, consequently, the *alcabala* will be owed to the tax collector who happens to be in office when the deed is fulfilled.[16]

In the barter as well as in the buy-sell operation, when both parties agree that for the contract to be considered complete and perfect the deed is needed, the contract shall be postponed by mutual agreement until the deed's execution.[17] In Castile, if before entering into the contract or at the moment of entering it somebody mentions the need of executing the deed, the contract is considered interrupted until the deed completes it. Argument 337 expounded on the same issue, regarding the contract of buying, unless from the concurrent circumstances in the case it is possible to surmise that the contracting parties had a different thing in mind, such as considering the deed only as proof and guaranty of the contract. Lassarte, however, warns us in the text cited above that, because the delivery is necessary to complete the

14. D. 19.4.1.

15. Cod. 4.64.3.

16. Gómez, *Opus*, t. 2, c. 2, no. 17.

17. Cod. 4.21.17. This is affirmed by Lassarte, *De decima venditionis et permutationis*, c. 17, no. 47, and the doctors usually.

barter, mere intent is not enough to consider the barter contract complete, even if it proceeds from both parties.

When the barter contract is interrupted, until the deed is executed common law and Castilian law allow both parties to change their minds and withdraw from the contract before the deed is executed, even if one of the parties had already delivered the good. Also, if the contract were to be executed, the tax should be paid to the tax collector in office at the moment of executing the deed, because it is then that the contract is deemed complete. Such is Lassarte's[18] opinion, which furthermore is evident.

Lassarte[19] judges correctly that no tax should be paid for contracts such as the following: I give you a certain good so that you give it to Peter after a certain period of time, or I give you 100 units so that you give John 50, or I give you a certain piece of property that I own so that you pay me or someone else a certain rent. His reason is that in order to pay taxes for the contract we call *do ut des*, it is necessary for the things reciprocally being delivered to be different, and one cannot be included in the other, nor can its fruits or the rights that derive from it. But even if Lassarte may judge all these contracts to be innominate, such as the one we call *do ut des*, I would prefer saying they are different forms of donation. And we know that donations are not subject to the *alcabala*, as they belong to a very different kind of contract from the one of sale and of barter in their strict sense.[20]

Everyone agrees that when a good of a certain kind is handed over for another of a different kind, such as a horse for an ox, wheat for oil, and so forth, or an individual of a species for another of the same species but of a different value, as would be one horse for another, it is a barter and, as such, we all know that the double tax should be paid. It is uncertain, however, whether

18. Lassarte, *De decima venditionis et permutationis*, c. 17, no. 47.

19. Lassarte, *De decima venditionis et permutationis*, c. 17, no. 7.

20. Argument 382, on the sale of real property, which is subject to payment of annual payments secured by a census on the property (*censo reservativo*), and on the *alcabala*.

when a certain individual of a specific species is handed over in exchange for another of the same species and similar value, as would be a certain measure of wheat for another of equal amount, or a measure of wine or oil for another that is equal, it should be considered a barter or not, and whether the tax should be paid. Parladorius, together with Bartolus and several others,[21] believe it should be considered a *mutuo*, because of which no tax should be paid. Lassarte seems to hold a better opinion[22] when he says that it is important to take into account whether, given the circumstances, the individuals intend to carry out a *mutuo*, as may be considered from the way of entering into the contract and the circumstances in which it is carried out, and in such case no tax is owed. This happens, for example, when someone borrows wheat, wine, oil, even a ram, or similar things, which have to be paid later by giving back an individual of the same species and of a more or less similar value. They could also attempt a contract that is different from the bartering contract, as would be a deposit or consignment of a dowry that is to be returned once the marriage is dissolved. And neither at that time should the tax be paid, even if the depositary has used up the good that was deposited and has to pay up somewhere else delivering a similar good. Finally, given the circumstances and way of entering into the contract, the conclusion might be that the individuals want to execute a barter and, in that case, they should pay the tax even if they tried concealing the barter under the pretext of a *mutuo*.

There is no certain rule allowing us to know whether what is being carried out is a barter that benefits the individuals, because if someone who owns wheat somewhere else requests in the very same place where he is that a friend lend him wheat for daily use, and this friend lends it so that it is rendered back when

21. Parladorius, *De rerum quotidianarum*, no. 33.

22. Lassarte, *De decima venditionis et permutationis*, c. 17, no. 9; N. R. 9.17.2.

the other receives the wheat in this very same place, it should be considered a *mutuo* and not a barter. Likewise, if someone asked for a loan of wheat to pay it later with the harvest obtained from it, it should be considered not a barter but a *mutuo*, even if it is convenient to the one who grants it. However, if someone delivered wheat in the place where he is so that the same quantity is paid back in some other place where he may sell it for a higher price, it shall be considered a barter even if they try to conceal it as a *mutuo*, unless the circumstances suggest that the one who received the wheat requested and received it as a loan. So too if there were two people who lived in different places and each had wheat where the other one lived, it would be considered a barter even if they wanted to cover it up as a *mutuo*.

All these issues make it worthwhile to entrust oneself to a prudent person who, once having examined the concurrent circumstances in a case, shall judge if it is a barter or a *mutuo*.

In the event that two goods are bartered, it is the responsibility of the judge or whomever he designates,[23] to appraise both in order to estimate the tax amount. That is why it should not be appraised according to the value established by the parties, even if the barter contract indicates the value of the goods that are bartered. If initially a good was sold for its price and later both parties decided by common agreement that instead of paying the price they shall pay by delivering another good, it shall not be considered a barter but a double sale, and the tax should be paid according to the price stipulated for each one of them.[24]

When a good cannot be sold because its value is considered inestimable, such as would be the right to burial and many other things that were discussed in argument 340 and in several others, the barter of this good for another that can be priced shall

23. N. R. 9.17.2.

24. Arias Pinel, *Ad rubricam et legem secundam C. de rescindenda venditione commentarii* (Salamanca, 1568), part. 2, c. 1, no. 16; Lassarte, *De decima venditionis et permutationis*, c. 17, no. 17.

not be subject to a tax for either of the goods. In fact, because it is a sacred good, of inestimable value, no tax should be paid, nor does the law cited above apply.[25] Moreover, just as the sale of such goods is considered invalid because of simony, so too shall the barter for a profane good be considered invalid; and we know that for an invalid sale or barter no *alcabala* should be paid. For this same reason, the *alcabala* should not be paid in the opposite case either, that is, when a profane good is bartered for another good considered of inestimable value. On the other hand, even if spiritual goods[26] may be bartered among them and lay people barter them, as happens with the right to burial and the chapels, no tax should be paid because they are goods of inestimable value.[27]

In this Castilian kingdom there are many things that are free of *alcabala*, such as books, horses supplied with bit and saddle, and many others.[28] When anyone interchanges any of these goods such as, for example, books for cinnamon, the person who interchanges the books is exempt from paying the *alcabala*. These things are considered privileged when they take the place of merchandise, so that the *alcabala* is neither owed for the price received for them, nor for the goods that, as a price, are received in exchange. However, the person who barters the cinnamon for the books must pay the *alcabala* according to the estimated value of books, because books are not considered privileged when they take the place of the price paid for the other goods, as should be evident. This is easy to prove, as the reference to law establishes money to be free of *alcabala* when it takes the place of merchandise, as happens with exchanging in a strict sense; but it is not considered so when it takes the place of price since, in this case, money does not free from the *alcabala* the good for

25. N. R. 9.17.2.

26. Cod. 4.64.3.

27. Lassarte, *De decima venditionis et permutationis*, c. 17, no. 18.

28. N. R. 9.17.2.

which that money is paid, but on the contrary, the seller pays the tax proportionate to the price.[29]

When a good is sold for an amount of money and, jointly, for another good, even if this good is of a much inferior value than that of the money, the Castilian law[30] orders both things to be jointly appraised by the judge, or by whom he designates, and the seller of the highest valued good should pay the *alcabala* for the total amount of the good plus the money he receives as payment, while the other individual must pay only for the value of the good he delivers. Thus, for example, if Peter sells a property to John for 1,000 gold coins plus a mule, and the latter's value is estimated to be 100 gold coins, Peter would have to pay an *alcabala* worth 1,100 gold coins. And even if the property is priced in 1,100 gold coins, John would only have to pay for the 100 coins the mule he delivers is worth.[31]

It is evident that the donation handed over as reward does not pay *alcabala* in Castile or Portugal, since it is not a barter, even if it is a reward for a good and not for a service. What happens is that the donations handed over as reward are not owed out of justice as happens in bartering, but originate from the individual's gratitude and generosity. And it is irrelevant that the law[32] says it should be considered a special kind of barter, since it does not confirm that it is a barter but as having a certain likeness to it, that is, as reward for a benefit that was previously received.[33]

If the donation were reciprocal between the individuals, it shall be considered a barter, and the *alcabala* shall have to be paid. However, if when the situation is considered from a general standpoint and not from the simple act of delivery, and the reciprocal donation is seen to originate in the love and generosity

29. Lassarte, *De decima venditionis et permutationis*, c. 17, no. 19.

30. N. R. 9.17.2.

31. Lassarte, *De decima venditionis et permutationis*, c. 17, no. 20.

32. D. 5.3.25.11.

33. Lassarte, *De decima venditionis et permutationis*, c. 17, no. 53.

that the individuals feel for each other, the conclusion may be that it is a donation as long as the circumstances persuade us that the individuals wanted to make a donation. Otherwise, we would be dealing with a barter under the guise of a donation and, in that case, the double *alcabala* should be paid.

Because when exchanging in a strict sense both parties interchange money, and this is considered a privileged good regarding the payment of the *alcabala*, it is clear that the *alcabala* should not be paid for the exchange operations.

ARGUMENT 398

ON EXCHANGE IN A STRICT SENSE AND ITS TYPES

IS THE EXCHANGE DEALER'S ACTIVITY LICIT?

To exchange, in a strict sense as we already pointed out in argument 396, is no less than to trade money for money, and it is not necessary for the money exchanged to be different from the one received as far as the material, shape, or engraved seal on the coins. This is in spite of Juan de Medina's opinion.[1] Because, as Soto[2] believes, if the money were handed over in one place to be paid or handed back somewhere else, it shall be a real exchange, even if the money to be paid back is no different from the one received as far as the material or the seal.

Even if the parties who carry out the barter in the sense described in argument 397 have the same name[3] and both may be equally called barterer and barteree, they are not called the same in the exchange, nor do they carry out the same occupation, because the person who is asked for the exchange may rent

1. Juan de Medina, *De cambiis* (Salamanca, 1550), q. 1.

2. Domingo de Soto, *De iustitia et iure, libri decem* (Salamanca, 1553), lib. 6, q. 8, a. 1.

3. D. 19.4.1.

out the services and ability requested of him and for this he may justly charge something more than the amount he exchanges, as shall be evident for what we shall proceed to explain. For this reason, in order to make a distinction between both parties involved in the exchange, they are given different names: the person to whom the exchange is requested and who lends his services and resourcefulness by someone else's request is called an exchange dealer, especially if he holds the office in a public condition. He is also called *numulario*, *trapezita*, *collybista*, and *argentarius*, although some of these names may sometimes have a broader meaning. See Covarrubias[4] for further discussion on this issue. In Spanish he is called *vanquero*[5] [*sic*]. Conrado[6] calls the person who solicits the exchange *campsarius*. Medina and others give him the same name, because just as the borrower is one who receives a loan, the donee is one who receives a donation, and the legatee is one to whom a legacy is bequeathed, so also he who receives money in exchange is called an exchange dealer (*campsario*).

Is it licit to work as an exchange dealer in order to earn a profit? It must be said that it is an activity that is dangerous in itself, more dangerous than the activity of the person who does business and looks to earn a profit by buying, bartering, or selling; it is an activity not suitable for some people, such as the members of the clergy who are forbidden to engage in it. But, in spite of all this, if it is carried out as we describe below, it shall not be condemned as unjust or illicit. What is more, it may be practiced meritoriously, as said in argument 339 of those who carry out both bartering and buying and selling, seeing that both economic activities are useful to the republic, as we shall see from what we say below.

4. Diego de Covarrubias y Leyva, *De collatione veterum nummismatum* (Venice, 1581), c. 7, in princ. ad finem no. 4.

5. Ed. note: *vanquero* becomes *banquero*: banker.

6. Conrado de Summenhart, *Opus septipartitum de contractibus* (Hannover, 1500), q. 99; Medina, *De cambiis*, q. 1.

We shall not discuss the type of exchange where there is no desire to profit, as when coins of a higher value are exchanged for others of a lower value but that as a whole are equal in value both legally and in the people's common assessment. There is no uncertainty whatsoever in these types of contracts; we shall refer to the exchange that seeks a profit.

The type of exchange that seeks a profit and where a difference is perceived in the value of what is given and what is received may fall into one of three categories, disregarding for now whether the exchange is licit or illicit. Because the exchange is not carried out if the coins are not different, there may be a difference in the coins themselves, such as being made of a different material, having a different legal seal, or having both a different material and legal seal; a difference as far as the place, because the coins are given in one place to be returned in another (for example, given in Lisbon to be returned in Seville or Rome); or a difference as far as time, because they are given at a certain point in time to be returned at another. According to these three ways of specifying the difference, there are three types of exchange.

The first type of exchange is that in which the coins are exchanged because of the difference between the coins themselves. This is commonly called petty exchange because in it coins of a greater value are usually exchanged for coins of inferior value. It is also known as manual exchange, as some people describe it, because it is practiced from hand to hand in one and the same place.

The second type is an exchange in which the money is exchanged due to its different value in places that are also different. And because it is usually carried out through bills of exchange that instruct the money to be paid somewhere else, it is usually called exchange for bills of exchange (*cambium per litteras*).

The third type is that in which money is exchanged because of a difference in its value over time. This type of operation may be called exchange, but it lacks precision because, if looked upon closely, we do not find anything here but a loan; and if either one of the two individuals should receive anything more than the amount exchanged he would commit usury, unless the contract could be justified by reason of *lucrum cessans* ("profit ceasing"), *damnum emergens* ("loss occurring"), or any other legitimate ruling. This is why I said before that I was not considering whether the exchange was licit or illicit, so that this type of exchange would be included in the concept of exchange. We will proceed to discuss it in order to admit or condemn it if such were the case.

Generally, in the exchanges attention should always be paid to whether something more than the capital is received for the time difference, because whatever is received for reason of a time difference is usury and is unjustly received, as it is received for reason of the loan that formally or virtually is carried out in that deal, unless it is justified for reason of profit ceasing or any another legitimate justification.

It is worth noting that the three previously mentioned types of exchange appear at times combined, because in the case of coins that are different between each other, there may be a difference due to place, making the deal for which they are exchanged both an exchange of different coins and an exchange in which the places are also different. The difference due to place usually goes together with the difference of the moment in time when the money is to be returned, as they are usually places that are very distant between each other.

Soto admits a fourth type of exchange;[7] that is, one that is practiced because of the difference in value that a same kind of currency has in different places. Even if for the same coins—the *ducats*, for example—the same number of silver coins may be given in Flanders as in Spain, or in the New World, they would be worth more in Flanders than in Spain, and in Spain more than in the New World, due to a lesser amount of this type of coin. For this reason, more goods may be bought in Flanders than in Spain, and more in Spain than in the New World. I believe, however,

7. Soto, *De iustitia et iure*, lib. 6, q. 8, a. 2.

that it is not necessary to admit this fourth type of exchange, as the difference pointed out originates from the very different circumstances that exist in places that are so distant one from the other. This problem shall be sufficiently explained when we describe the reasons that make it licit in the exchange to receive something more than what the exchange dealer gave because of the difference of value between one place and another.

Navarrus distinguishes seven types of exchange, of which only some of them include rulings or justifications for the exchange dealer to licitly receive something more than the money given.[8] But there is no need to multiply the types of exchange; it shall be sufficient while explaining the types of exchange suggested here to examine the rulings that make it licit or not to receive something more than what was given. Moreover, it shall be sufficient to explain the petty exchange and the exchange that takes place because of the difference in places, and, at the same time, to analyze other rulings that make it licit or not to receive any increment over the capital.

The doctors also divide the exchanges into real and dry exchange, calling real exchange that which is true exchange and which allows drawing something more than the capital that is exchanged; and calling dry exchange that which is not true exchange, and thus not allowing to draw either more than the capital exchanged—that is, when in the exchange an increment is received only for the delay in time, which constitutes usury. The name *dry*, or *lacking in sap*, means it cannot produce fruit or profit. This is the sense in which these words are used in Pius V's bull on exchanges. Some use dry exchange to describe the exchange that is carried out when the exchange dealer hands over some money first to get it back with an increase at a later date, even if this retrieval is in a distant place. I believe this

8. Martín de Azpilcueta, *Manual de confesores y penitentes* (Salamanca, 1556), cap. 17, no. 286; Azpilcueta, *Comentario resolutorio de usuras* (Salamanca, 1556), no. 10.

name also results from the same previously declared notion, that is, that such exchange was considered in itself unfruitful and usurious, because of which no profit or increase could be licitly drawn from it, as the doctors affirm and the Portuguese ordinances[9] set down. But we shall examine this problem further on, and we shall prove that such definition was made without grounds. Navarrus says that these doctors call it dry because in it the exchange dealer gives the money before receiving it,[10] but I prefer what I have previously argued.

Medina and Conrado also divide the exchanges into pure and impure,[11] calling pure the exchange that is not mixed with any other type of contract and calling impure that which is mixed with another contract, including that of a loan, rent of the exchange dealer's services, or other similar ones. According to Soto in the second article cited earlier, it is more expressive to call the just exchange pure and the unjust one impure.

We have said all this to better understand the doctors, who in this matter usually express themselves in different ways.

9. *Ordenações Manuelinas*, lib. 4, tit. 14, § antepenúlt.

10. Azpilcueta, *Manual*, cap. 17, no. 286; Azpilcueta, *Comentario*, no. 10.

11. Medina, *De cambiis*, q. 2; Conrado, *Opus septipartitum de contractibus*, q. 99, suppositione 5.

Argument 399

Is It Licit for the Exchange Dealer to Receive in the Petty Exchange an Increment over the Price That the Law Has Appraised the Coins For?

It is clearly evident that petty exchange is useful to the republic, as it is often that men need coins of a lesser value in order to buy the things they need daily, or to give alms, or for other such things in which the coinage of a higher value is of no use. Conversely, those who wish to put away a great sum of money or take it elsewhere need to exchange small coins for larger ones and, likewise, those who emigrate to a place where the coins of their own land are of no value need to exchange them for others that are valuable wherever they go. For these and other purposes, the republic finds it useful to have exchange dealers who have access to diverse types of coins at the right time in order to exchange them with those who need them.

Once this is established, together with the doctors' common opinion we go on to say the following: just as with the contract of sale and all other commutative contracts in which it is necessary to abide by the equality between what is given and what is received in order for these contracts to be fair and for there to be no obligation of giving back, so in the exchange in which money is given for money should there be equality, because this is the law that rules over commutative contracts, among which is the exchange.

But money has a value that has been fixed by law, because of which, from this point of view, its value is indivisible both for the one who offers it as well as for the one who asks for it. The question now is, mainly, what rulings or grounds allow the exchanger to justly receive something more than the equivalent of what he gives, taking into account the appraised value of the coins being exchanged.

We must say, together with the doctors' common opinion, that exchange dealers may licitly receive a just price for the service they carry out, either from the republic or from those people who ask for the exchange when the republic does not pay them, as long as that price is not unwarranted in relation to the services rendered. If the price were unwarranted, there would be obligation to give back the excess charged above the rigorous just price of the service rendered. The services rendered by the exchange dealer are: getting together and having the coins of diverse types ready for those who wish to exchange them; being present for their services, whether it is themselves or someone else, at the public place of exchanges waiting for those who want to exchange; counting the money they give and the one they receive, and other such things. All these services deserve a fair retribution.

In this kingdom of Castile, anyone can undertake the public office of exchange dealer without any charge whatsoever. However, they must be elected in the royal court by the king himself. In other places they are elected by the judges and rulers of the city or town in which they are to practice their duties.[1] Under the above cited law 4 in statute 18, they are allowed to receive 4 *maravedis* for the exchange of 1 *castellano*; 3 *maravedis* for the exchange of 1 *dobla* or 1 *ducat*; 2 *maravedis* for the exchange

1. N. R. 5.18.1.

of 1 *florin*, and the same is said of the *ducat*.[2] Navarrus recalls that in Salamanca, at the time when he taught in that illustrious university, there was a public exchange dealer who used to charge 1 *maravedi* for the exchange of each *ducat*.[3]

In Portugal, they forbid that—for giving or receiving gold coins that are valuable in this kingdom, coined here or elsewhere—any plus or increment should be received above the just value of these;[4] and there is a penalty depriving the person of the coins' value, half of which is awarded to the accuser and half to the redemption of captives, along with the penalty of a two-year exile in Africa, excepting the case where one would have been appointed by the king as public exchange dealer of a place, allocating a certain fee to him. In that case he would be able to receive the increment licitly; but if he had not been allocated any fee whatsoever, he would not be able to receive anything and shall be subject to the same penalties as the others, despite the royal appointment. However, since the fee the exchange dealer receives justly is not received for the money he gives but for the service he renders, it is reasonable to believe that there are actually two contracts in the exchange, and both of them just: one, the exchange of money for money of the same value; the other, the hiring of the exchange dealer's services, for which he collects that just increment. As said in argument 304, following the opinion of Navarrus, Medina, Major, and others, in a loan the lender may not collect anything for the loan apart from the capital, but he may, because of the very nature of the problem (*ex ipsa natura rei*), collect a moderate stipend for the job of counting the money and for other services the exchange dealer does. Likewise, he may also collect a moderate stipend for the services mentioned before.

---

2. N. R. 5.21.62.

3. Martín de Azpilcueta, *Comentario resolutorio de usuras* (Salamanca, 1556), cap. final.

4. *Leis extravagantes*, part. 4, tit. 11, law 4, § 9.

It is uncertain whether the private exchange dealers, who have not been appointed by the republic to carry out this duty, may also receive an increment for the responsibilities they carry out in favor of those who ask for an exchange, such as counting the money and other tasks they perform. Cajetan denies this in his *opusculum* on exchange[5] because, in the first place, he says that counting the money does not deserve a payment, as it has always been done for free; in the second place, because sometimes the person who seeks the exchange counts a larger amount of money than the exchanger; third, because the exchanger's action of counting is the same as the action carried out by the person who seeks the exchange. But the common opinion of the doctors declares quite the opposite, that is, that private exchange dealers, the same as the official exchanger, may also licitly collect, because of the nature of the problem (*ex natura rei*), a small increment for the action of counting or other similar services rendered, in much the same way as the official exchanger. But what they may licitly collect should be less than what the public exchange dealers collect, because the public exchange dealers' duty takes up many more expenses and work, as he has declared above. Thus, acknowledge Medina (although, at first glance, he seems to suggest otherwise in the penultimate paragraph of the preceding question 1.a), Soto, Navarrus, Conrado, Biel, Silvestre, and others.[6] The reason is

5. Tomás de Vio Cajetan, *De cambiis* (Milan, 1499), tract. 7, caps. 1, 6.

6. Juan de Medina, *De cambiis* (Salamanca, 1550), q. 2 and q. 1, § penúlt; Domingo de Soto, *De iustitia et iure, libri decem* (Salamanca, 1553), lib. 6, q. 9; Martín de Azpilcueta, *Manual de confesores y penitentes* (Salamanca, 1556), cap. 17, no. 288; Azpilcueta, *Comentario*, no. 19; Conrado de Summenhart, *Opus septipartitum de contractibus* (Hannover, 1500), q. 99, concl. 5; Gabriel Biel, *Commentarii doctissimi in IV sententiarum libros* (Brescia, 1574), dist. 15, q. 11, a. 3, dub. 12; John Major, *In quartum sententiarum quaestiones utilissimae* (Paris, 1521), q. 37; Diego de Covarrubias y Leyva, *De collatione veterum nummismatum* (Venice, 1581), cap. 7, no. 4, in prin.; Silvestre de Prierias, *Sylvestrina summa, qua summa summarum merito nuncupatur* (Lyons, 1555), verb. usura, t. 4, q. 7, pronunc. 3.

that such service is worthy of remuneration, even if it is meager, because of which the first argument should be denied, which is the one that persuaded Cajetan. To the second argument we respond that even if the exchange dealer counts the money he gives as well as the money he receives, both things are carried out at the request of the person seeking the exchange, because of which both acts of counting should be paid, just as the lender should be remunerated for the service of counting, both when he gives the loan and when it is returned to him, as both actions are carried out for the borrower's benefit and he could refuse them if he did not wish to carry out the service of lending. That is why it should be denied, in the third argument, that one job is compensated with another, as this does not happen either in the case of the loan, because in both cases all the work is carried out for the benefit of the one seeking the loan or the exchange.

All this explanation should be considered correct in accordance with the nature of the problem (*ex natura rei*), because the republic could forbid drawing for the exchanges an amount that is greater than the value of the exchanged coins, and this on account of the republic's own good, in order to prevent the increment in the price of coins, and to prevent foreigners from carrying gold or silver out of the country, offering for them a much better price, all of which would be detrimental to the republic.

Soto says in the place already referred to, in the third conclusion, that in this kingdom there has already been a law that forbids anyone, excluding the public exchange dealers appointed by the republic, from collecting an increment over the exchanges. Quite the opposite, Navarrus says, in the already quoted number 19, that even if in this kingdom it is forbidden to carry out the responsibilities of a public exchanger as a result of one's own decision, it is not, however, forbidden to exchange to private persons, nor collecting for it a profit, and he quotes the laws that resolve it. He complains that Soto does not quote the law that backs his opinion. Covarrubias, in the quoted work, embraces

Soto's opinion and quotes the current laws[7] in favor of it. But in these laws there is only a prohibition to carry out the duties of a public exchanger in the Court without having been appointed by the king, or by the judge or rulers in other places; but they do not forbid all the rest from carrying out exchanges in private.

Perhaps it is considered forbidden for private individuals to collect an increment for petty exchange because of the laws that today appraise gold coins (which we shall discuss shortly), which forbid collecting any increment, as Gutiérrez holds.[8] We have already said that this is the legislation in Portugal, but I believe that in neither of the two kingdoms is anything regularly collected for petty exchange.

I would like to caution that what Soto and Covarrubias declare—that is, that once the law that prohibits collecting anything for petty exchange is promulgated there is obligation to restitute if anything were received—is a complex issue, as we could be dealing here with the just price received for the service involved in the exchange. For even if the prince might forbid in this case such increment on account of the republic's common good, and in law it is enough for a ruling to forbid something so that if it is done the contract is nullified and invalidated;[9] however, in the present case, it would be the just compensation derived *ex natura rei* between what is received and the good for which something is received. Also, from what we said in argument 88, especially when confirming the first argument, the rulings not subject to what the law has ordered in the cited place do not prevent the individual from receiving his just reward. That is why I believe that by violating these rulings only a sin of disobedience to the prince is committed; a disobedience that *ex genere suo* is by no means serious. And if what was received exceeded *ex natura rei*

7. N. R. 5.18.1.

8. Juan Gutiérrez, *Practicarum quaestionum circa Leges Regias Hispaniae* (Salamanca, 1589), lib. 2, q. 178.

9. Cod. 1.14.5.

the limits of the just stipend, then the sin would certainly be *ex genere suo* serious, as a greater increment than what is just would have been received, there being obligation to restitute.

There is another resolution by which the private individuals may licitly obtain a profit, namely, when in the place where the exchange takes place they give for the exchanged money less than what it is worth, not in that place but in a different one, and then the individuals take the money to that other place, or they exchange it to travelers who are going there for the value it has over there, because they wish to do this favor without incurring any loss for themselves. Thus, the residents in a country usually do business by exchanging money from other kingdoms without any value in the place where the exchange is being carried out, for a low amount. In order to do this, they buy money from other countries that lacks value in the place where the exchange is taking place, and thus they buy it cheap licitly since it is not worth anything in that country; then they take the money bought like this to a place where it has a value appraised by law, or they exchange it with travelers who are going to that place for the value it has in that country. Medina, Cajetan, and others[10] agree with this. Notice, however, that sometimes the price is so low that it does not equal the value of the coins' metal (for example, Portuguese silver coins). In that case, it would be unjust, and there would be obligation to restitute the amount lacking for the lowest just price. Because if the price paid for the coins were below the price of the silver sold in ingots, the contract would certainly be unjust and there would be obligation to restitute.

10. Medina, *De cambiis*, q. 9 § últ.; Cajetan, *De cambiis*, cap. 6.

Argument 400

On Diverse Gold and Silver Coins That Have Been Coined in Castile and Portugal over Time

On Their Value at the Moment of Coinage and at the Present Time

On the Value of Gold and Silver Ingots in These Kingdoms at Different Times

In order to better understand what we need to say on exchanges, we should discuss the matters indicated in the title of this argument, as we are more familiar with the coins from Castile and Portugal than with those from other kingdoms. All things considered, what we say about those from Castile and Portugal shall make it easy to surmise what should be considered about the other coins, once we have the information about the laws that refer to them and their characteristics.

For a better understanding, take into account that a half pound (*selibra*) of gold and silver, which the Spanish call *marco*, and in other places *marca*, is a coin that weighs 8 ounces; and the ounce is divided into 8 eighths, which the Hebrews call *adharcon*, and the Greeks and Latins call *drachmas*. The Spanish, distorting the Greco-Roman name, call it *drama*, *adarame*, or *adarme*. I suspect that, as happens with many words in our language, *adarame* is a word that the Spanish inherited from the Saracens who occupied the Spanish territories, and whose language is very similar to the Hebrew tongue. In this kingdom of Castile they call the half *ochavo*[1]—namely, the sixteenth part of an ounce—a *dram* or *adarame*, and so the half pound contains 64 *ochavos*, as the 8 ounces in the half pound times 8 *ochavos* make 64 *ochavos*. The gold *ochavo* has 72 grains.

Consider that to express the degree of purity or impurity of gold, the goldsmiths divide the half pound, or any other quantity of gold, into 24 parts, which they call *caractos*, and in Spanish, *quilates* ("carats"). Alternatively, each carat is divided into fourths, into eighths of a carat, and into other similar proportional parts—some bigger and some smaller. When the gold is very pure and not mixed with any other metal, it is said to be 24-carat, because the half pound, or any other weight of that gold, has 24 parts of gold and none of any other metal. And this is the gold they call *obryzo*, which in Greek means "sincere" and "delicate." Others believe the name comes from Ophir, but the etymology is uncertain. When a half pound of gold has 23 parts of gold and 1 part from another metal (silver, copper, or whatever it may be), it is said to be 23-carat gold. When 22 parts of gold are mixed with 2 parts of another metal, it is said to be 22-carat gold, and so on and so forth. Likewise, to express the purity or impurity of silver they divide the half pound (or any other mass) into 12 parts, called *denarios* (*denari*). Thus, when the half pound of silver is not mixed with any other metal but is pure silver, it is called 12-*denari* silver; and when 11 parts of silver are mixed with 1 part of another metal it is called 11-*denari* silver, and is said by the Spanish to have one *denari* of *liga*,[2] and consequently it is estimated to be silver of less *denari*, the more *denari* of another metal are mixed into it. The *denari*, in turn, is divided into 24 parts, each of which is called a grain of silver. Thus, this grain of silver weighs much less than the grain of gold.

1. Ed. note: *ochavo* means both "one eighth" and is the name of the Spanish copper coin weighing an eighth of an ounce and worth 2 *maravedis*.

2. Ed. note: *liga*: mix, blend.

Also consider that in this kingdom of Castile, according to Covarrubias' account,[3] King Ferdinand and his wife, Queen Isabella,[4] ordered minting 23¾-carat gold *ducats*, hence, each of these was only one-fourth of a carat short of being gold of the highest purity. This tiny part of metal was mixed with the gold to give it a greater consistency, as gold of the highest purity lacks solidity and bends too easily. The half pound was worked into 65⅓ *ducats*, making each *ducat* contain an eighth of an ounce of gold, taking from each of the 64 *ducats* as many grains as necessary to fabricate one more *ducat* and a third of another in order to cover the mintage expenses, which made each *ducat* contain less than one-eighth of an ounce of gold, almost 1½ grains less. These same kings ordered the issuing of a coin worth twice the value of a *ducat*, from that gold, which in this kingdom they call *dobla*, and another worth one-fifth of the *ducat*, called *quíntupla*, another they call *décupla*, and others worth 20 and 50 *aúreos*.[5]

In this kingdom, the *ducat* is worth 11 silver *reales* and 1 *maravedi*, and the silver *real* is worth 34 *maravedis*, because of which the *ducat* contains 375 *maravedis* (11 × 34 + 1). This is the reason why they estimate that one-half pound in this type of gold ingot was worth 24,000 *maravedis*, as 64 × 375 = 24,000, allocating toward minting expenses an extra 1⅓ *ducat* struck from the half pound.[6] But the *ducats* produced with a half pound were worth 24,500 *maravedis*, because the 1⅓ *ducat* that was taken for expenses from the 64 eighths of an ounce used for producing the other 64 *ducats* was worth 500 *maravedis*.

From what has been said, it is easy to surmise, in the first place, the reason why 1 *maravedi* was added to the 11 silver

3. Diego de Covarrubias y Leyva, *De collatione veterum nummismatum* (Venice, 1581), cap. 3, no. 2, in princ.; no. 2 § 1; N. R. 5.21.1.

4. Ed. note: This is a reference to the monetary policy promulgated by King Ferdinand II of Aragón (1452–1516) and Queen Isabella (1451–1504) in Medina del Campo in 1497.

5. Ed. note: *aúreo*: gold coin.

6. N. R. 5.21.4.

reales of a *ducat*'s price: so that the half pound of that gold was given a value of 24,000 *maravedis* and each *ducat* had a gold *drachma*, taking away from each of the 64 *ducats* the grains that were needed to produce 1⅓ *ducats* for minting expenses. We understand too that the Gospel's *drachmas* weighed the same as our *ducats* or silver *reales*, as we shall see from the following, as in order to prove this you only need to add to the gold and silver coins what was taken from each *drachma* for expenses. They are called *drachmas* because of the coin's weight, but they were silver and not gold. And the *didrachma* which, as also mentioned in the Gospel, was paid as tax, weighed 2 *drachmas* and was worth 2 silver *reales*. In the third place, we may surmise that at the time when those *ducats* were minted, the gold grain was worth almost 5¼ *maravedis*, because one-eighth of a gold ounce weighs 72 grains, which, at the rate of 5 *maravedis* per grain, amounts to 360 *maravedis*. And the 15 *maravedis* needed to complete 375 have 60-fourths of *maravedi*, so that in order for the gold grain to be worth in those 5¼ *maravedis*, they only needed twelve-fourths of *maravedi*.

In time, that extremely pure gold became highly coveted in other countries and was taken out of the Spanish territories. This is why, as Covarrubias[7] says, Charles V[8] ordered the mintage of

7. Covarrubias, *De collatione veterum nummismatum*, cap. 3, no. 2, in princ.; no. 4, § 1; N. R. 5.21.10.

8. Ed. note: Charles I of Hapsburg (1500–1558), who later became Emperor Charles V of the Holy Roman Empire. As the son of Philip the Handsome, Duke of Burgundy, and Joanna, third child of Ferdinand of Aragón and Isabella of Castile, he was heir presumptive to an empire vaster than Charlemagne's, and over which the "sun never set." The empire included the Netherlands and claims to the Burgundian circle; it included Castile, Aragón, the conquered kingdoms of Navarre and Granada, Naples, Sicily, Sardinia, the conquests of the New World, and possessions in North Africa, all of which after the death of Ferdinand he ruled jointly with his mad mother; and it included the Hapsburg duchies of Austria with rights over Hungary and Bohemia, inherited from his paternal grandfather, Emperor Maximilian I. The main objective of his reign was not new conquest but

22-carat gold coins, which were called *coronas* or *escudos*. Sixty-eight *escudos* weigh the same as a half pound, and the value of each *escudo* is 10 *reales* and 10 *maravedis* or, the equivalent, 350 *maravedis*. And if you take away an *escudo* paid as duty to the king for each half pound, plus 1¾ *tomin* for the mintage, the value of a half pound struck from a 22-carat gold ingot amounts to 23,331 *maravedis*,[9] since the *tomin* has 12 grains of gold and is worth 2 silver *reales*, so that the *tomin* and three-fourths have 21 grains and are worth 3½ silver *reales*, that is, 119 *maravedis*. This amount, together with the *escudo*, whose value was at the 350 *maravedis*, amount to 469 *maravedis*. If these are subtracted from the 23,800 *maravedis*, the gold half pound produced out of that kind of ingot is worth 23,381 *maravedis*. The 23-carat gold half pound had 95-fourths of gold carat and one-fourth of another metal. The 22-carat gold half pound only had 88-fourths of gold carat and 8-fourths of another metal, because 23,331 *maravedis* divided by the 88-fourths of a carat equal 265¹⁄₁₁ *maravedis*. According to this calculation, this is the value of each carat. Consequently, a half pound of a 23¾-carat gold ingot, which has 7-fourths of a carat more, is worth, once the *escudos* have been minted, 25,186 *maravedis* plus 7-elevenths parts. And as the 22-carat gold half pound has 2 carats of *liga* ("blend"), of which two parts are silver and one part is copper, it follows that

---

the protection and consolidation of his inheritance, which he sought to accomplish through strategic matrimonial alliances. But, as it turns out, his reign would be plagued with international conflict that would eventually overcome him. The conflicts were exacerbated by the Lutheran Reformation in Germany. Shortly before his death, Charles' proposal of the succession of his son Philip to the imperial title was rejected at the Diet of Augsburg and that event, in conjunction with several other blows, led him to abdicate his office. He gave the governments of the Netherlands, Spain, and Sicily to Philip. To Ferdinand he handed over the Hapsburg Empire, but not the title of Emperor, which he retained until 1558 (*NCE*, 3:503–6, s.v. "Charles V, Holy Roman Emperor").

9. N. R. 5.21.46.

said 22-carat gold half pound has 1¾ carats of silver, as well as two-thirds carats of copper.

Therefore, as the silver half pound is worth in this kingdom 65 silver *reales*,[10] the silver carat shall have a value of 92 1/12 *maravedis*, and 1⅓ carats shall be worth almost 123 *maravedis*. If you subtract this amount from the 25,186, the 23¾-carat gold half pound is worth 20,066 *maravedis*, once the *escudos* have been minted. Thus, one-eighth of an ounce of this ingot is worth 391 39/64 *maravedis*. If you add 500 *maravedis* to this for minting expenses, you shall see that this was the value of 1 *ducat* in those times.

In the year 1566, King Philip II[11] raised the value of each *escudo* to 400 *maravedis*, without changing their weight or the amount of gold or silver in the blending, so that a half pound of *escudos* was worth 27,200 *maravedis*, which is their value today.[12] If you take away an *escudo* (worth today 400 *maravedis*) for the king's tax, plus 141 for expenses, which is what they pay today in Seville, where only 119 were paid before, the half pound of this gold ingot is worth 26,659 *maravedis*. And if they divide these between 88 highly pure gold carat quarts, which the half pound contains, as the other 8 are part of the *liga*, one-fourth of highly pure gold carat is worth almost 303 *maravedis*, as

10. N. R. 5.21.5.

11. Ed. note: Philip II (1527–1598), son of Charles I of Spain (the Emperor Charles V) and Isabella of Portugal, began his reign in 1543 as regent in Spain during his father's absence in Germany. In 1556 Philip succeeded to the throne, which included the crown of Castile with Navarre and the Indies, the crown of Aragón-Catalonia with Sardinia, and the crown of Sicily: a veritable world empire. But financial difficulties forced him to settle in Spain, impose his authority, and withdraw from the widespread commitments of his father. He distrusted subordinates and governed as an absolute monarch, but he always respected the autonomous status of the constituent kingdoms (*NCE*, 11:272–73, s.v. "Philip II, King of Spain"). Philip II's monetary policy originated in the parliamentary assembly of Madrid in 1566.

12. N. R. 5.21.13.

26,659 ÷ 88 = 302.943, and the 7-fourths of pure gold carat that are also contained in the 23¾-carat gold half pound are worth today almost 1,222 *maravedis*. For this reason the half pound of the gold with which the *ducats* are made, without discounting anything on account of the blend, is worth today around 27,900 *maravedis*. Today almost nothing is taken away on account of the blend, because, from what I have heard in Seville, it is copper and has no silver.

The eighth of an ounce of this mass is worth around 435 *maravedis*, that is 12 silver *reales* and 27 *maravedis*, the same as what the *ducat* of this mass is worth if you add 541 *maravedis* for minting expenses, which are used as compensation for what is lacking in gold in each one to complete the eighth of an ounce. But law 13 cited earlier ordered the *ducats* to be current at 429 *maravedis*, and we must abide by it. Perhaps there is something missing to explain this price difference, or perhaps, having used external help for the calculations (since I do not know arithmetic), something was erroneously calculated, but what I have just explained sheds no little amount of light on what we shall proceed to say.

I should point out three things. First, the Castilian goldsmiths and their helpers at the mint apply the principles disclosed on carats not to gold half pounds but to the gold of the coins called *castellanos*, worth 16 silver *reales* or 544 *maravedis*, if they are 22-carat. This is verified in the above-cited law 13. And they say that the *castellano*'s highly pure carat is worth today 24 *maravedis* plus some particles from another *maravedi*, and because 50 of these coins weigh a half pound, they find it very easy to use this coin as a measure for counting carats. Second, even if the silver mass is valued in this kingdom so that the half pound cannot exceed the price of 65 silver *reales*, no price is fixed for the gold mass, but only on the coins with which they are made, once they have discounted the cost of minting and the tax paid to the king. Third, the law forbids the goldsmiths from producing gold objects that are not 24-carats minus an eighth of a carat, or 22- or

20-carats.[13] And this same law establishes penalties for those who sell gold objects with fewer carats than the ones indicated.

In this same kingdom, Ferdinand and Isabella ordered the mintage of silver made out of 11 *denari* and 4 grains in the proportion of 67 silver *reales* per half pound, because of which they had 20 grains of blend with another metal, that is, copper.[14] It was worth 34 *maravedis*, as is manifest in law 4 of the same section. The half pound of this silver in ingots was valued so that it could not be sold for more than 65 silver *reales*, as is manifest in law 5 of the same section, and since 67 *reales* were minted from it, as states the same law and also the second law already cited, it follows that each *real* only had 32 silver *maravedis*. And since 1 *real* plus 1 *maravedi* are paid for the expenses of casting the half pound, as is manifest in law 46 from the same section and according to what was said by a public officer in the mint, it follows that the 33 extra *maravedis* are the profit of the person who gave the silver to produce the *ducats*. And this is specifically stated in law 5 of the same section.

The above has not been modified at all thus far, as is manifest in law 13 of the same section's declarations. There is only a difference in one point: that by a royal *cédula* sent to the mints in the territories of Spain a tribute of 50 *maravedis* was established to be paid to the king for each silver half pound that was minted in them. This tribute is called *señorage*. This is the reason why a person who coins a silver half pound only receives 64½ silver *reales*.

Almost at the same time that Ferdinand and Isabella ordered the *ducats* to be minted, similar coins were coined in Portugal with highly pure 24-carat gold, which we call here *cruzados*. The simple *cruzado*, or *ducat*, had an eighth of an ounce of gold, having taken three-fourths of a grain for expenses, as they had

13. N. R. 5.24.4. Ed. note: Cf. N. N. R. 9.10.19.

14. N. R. 5.21.2.

71¾ grains.[15] The 10 *ducat cruzado*, called *portugués* in that kingdom, had 11-eighths ounce and 64½ grains, lacking only 7½ grains for completing 10-eighths, as said in paragraph 3 of law 4 already cited. And since the *ducat* is worth 400 *reais* in that kingdom, it follows that the half pound of that gold ingot was estimated at the time in 25,600 *reais*. But the gold half pound, converted to those coins, was worth 25,800 *reais*, with an extra charge on account of the 48 grains that were taken for expenses from the 64 *ducats*, since at the time the gold grain was worth 5½ *reais* plus a part of a *septil*. Seventy-two grains, at the rate of 5 *reais*, make 360 *reais*. And if each one of the 40 *reais* left to complete the 400 are divided by 2 we obtain 80 halves. And if we take from there 72 halves for the 72 grains, each grain shall be worth 5½ *reais* plus 1/72 *reais*, which make 24 *septiles*.

In the time of Charles V, João III,[16] encouraged by the same reasons as the emperor, ordered the minting in Portugal of *ducats* called in this country *cruzados de cruz piquena*. Today they call them *cruzados do meio*, because they were coined during the time between the mintage of those first highly pure gold ones and others of an inferior purity. The gold of these was 22⅝-carat, and they only had a mix of 1¾-carat of another metal. Each one weighed 71¼, just as highly pure gold *ducats*. All this is contained in paragraph 5 of the already cited law 4.

Thus, since these *ducats* maintained the price of 400 *reais*, the half pound of impure gold began to be worth the same as what the half pound of that highly pure gold was worth before. Sub-

15. *Leis extravagantes*, part. 4, tit. 11, law 4, § 4.

16. Ed. note: The double marriage between the king of Portugal, João III (1521–1557) and Dona Catarina, sister of the Holy Roman Emperor Charles V, in 1525, and between João's sister Isabella and the Holy Roman Emperor in 1526, "constituted a stunningly prestigious diplomatic victory for Portugal and a testimony to its wealth. In the 1540s, a similar double marriage, between the crown princes of Portugal and Spain and their respective sisters, prepared the ground for the eventual union of Portugal and Hapsburg Spain in 1580" (*EtR*, 5:135, s.v. "Portugal").

sequently, João III ordered minting other *ducats* called *cruzados de cruz de monte calvario*, with 22⅛-carat gold. They weighed 72⅞ grains, because of which they only lacked one-eighth of a grain to complete the eighth of a gold ounce, as states paragraph 6 of the same law. That is why, since these *ducats* maintained the price of 400 *reais*, the half pound of this impure gold began to be worth the same as what the half pound of very pure gold was worth before.

Lately, King João III himself ordered the minting of a coin, which was the most commonly used in Portugal when I was teaching these subjects there. It was made with 22⅛-carat gold. Its weight was such that 30 coins weighed a half pound, and each was worth 1,000 *reais*, hence the name *moedas de mil reais*. They had other coins that weighed half as much, so that 60 weighed one-half pound and were worth 500 *reais*, and were called *moedas de quinientos reais*, as appears in paragraphs 8 and 9 of law 4 referred to earlier. Consequently, the half pound of very pure 24-carat gold was worth 25,600 *reais*, as has already been said. And when these new coins were coined, the half pound produced from the ingot of this much more impure 22⅛-carat gold began to be worth 30,000 *reais*. And the value of the highly pure gold coins increased in the same proportion, not only so that the price in coins of 1,000 *reais* would correspond to the same weight (at the rate of 30,000 *reais* per half pound), but so that a greater quantity of highly pure gold would correspond to a higher price in the same proportion in which the quantity of highly pure gold of the old coins exceeds the quantity contained in the 1,000 *reais* coins, subtracting something on account of the blend of other metals they contain, as was taken away from the coins from Castile. All of which is established in the *Leis extravagantes*, law 4 cited above, as we shall later declare.

Law 4 fixed that price for the new gold coins, and in paragraph 11 it forbade obtaining a profit when exchanging them and established a penalty of loss of the coins' value and two years of banishment in places in Africa. That is why the price fixed by the law was the current price. However, foreign merchants started offering 1,100 for the 1,000 *reais* coins and 550 for the coins of 500 *reais*. And suddenly, during the time in which I instructed on these subjects, many hurried to offer for that price great quantities of them with full knowledge of the Senate and other public officers, without anyone stopping them. Even those who were in charge of the government's finances and the king's assets did this. Perhaps what I will go on to describe contributed greatly to this.

The silver of coins from Portugal has only 11 *denarios*, that is, there is a whole *denari* of another metal mixed into it.[17] As a result, in Flanders, Germany, and other nations they are not worth more than the silver they contain, taking into account, besides, their impurity. King Sebastian[18] ordered in the cited law that from the half pound of this type of silver 24 *tostoes* were to be minted, worth 100 *reais* each. Therefore, the half pound was worth 2,400 *reais* or the equivalent 6 *cruzados*. Since those who brought silver in order to mint it did not pay but 60 *reais* for minting expenses, as the law orders, it follows that, in those times, the half pound of that type of silver was worth in ingots 2,340 *reais*. João III's grandfather had ordered minting 26 *tostoes* from the half pound of silver of that type and, because of this,

17. *Leis extravagantes*, part. 5, tit. 8, law 1.

18. Ed. note: Sebastian of Portugal (1554–1578) succeeded to the throne in 1557 following the death of Dom João III. Sebastian, a young child and grandson to Dom João III, now embodied all the hopes of the Avis dynasty. But Sebastian was chronically ill, both physically and mentally. Though he lived into adulthood, his weakness and unwillingness to leave an heir left considerable doubts about the dynasty's future. These doubts were realized in 1578 when Sebastian was killed in the battle of Alcacer Kebir (Qsar al-kabir), in an ill-conceived attempt to rekindle the Portuguese conquest in Morocco. His elderly great-uncle, Cardinal Dom Henrique, a caretaker king, proved unable to manage a smooth dynastic transition. A brief war of succession ensued in 1580, but Philip II of Spain met little resistance in laying claim to the throne of Portugal, which temporarily united Spain and Portugal (*EtR*, 5:135, s.v. "Portugal").

at the time of João III the half pound of these *tostoes* was worth 1,600 *reais*, that is, 6½ *cruzados*, as says the same law. Before João III the *tostoes* weighed more, but all the *tostoes* had a value of 100 *reais*, even if some had more silver and others less. What is more, King Sebastian ordered in the cited section's second law that the *tostoes* that João III had ordered minted maintain the same value, and that nobody could reject them when they were handed out to pay goods or debts. During all this time, the silver *real* was worth 36²⁄₇ *reais* in Portugal, so that 11 of them were worth 400 *reais*, that is, 1 *cruzado*. And King Sebastian, in the cited section, decreed in the year 1558 that this was their price and, under certain penalties, nobody should receive more for them.

At the time, in East India, the silver *real* was worth 60 *reais*, and in Africa it was worth 40 *maravedis*. They were much preferred everywhere and were used to negotiate, and not the Portuguese silver coins. And from the region of Ethiopia called Mina, they brought to Portugal a great amount of gold and delivered a lot of gold in exchange for silver coins. That is why in those times, without the referred to law being able to stop it, in order to send great quantities of them to the East Indies many bought silver *reales* for a price that was higher than the legal one. Even the king and his ministers did this. Everyone was concerned whether or not it was licit to buy them in Portugal for a higher price than the legal one. That was the situation while I taught these subjects and while King Sebastian was getting ready to go to Africa, the price of the silver *real* suddenly rose in Portugal to 40 *reais*, making 10 of them to begin to be worth 400 *reais*, that is, 1 *cruzado*. This was done without promulgating any law but, simply, because the king began to pay salaries and goods at that price, and the ministers of the king would force the private individuals to accept the silver *reales* at that same price. From then on, *tostoes* started being coined with a weight of 2½ *reales*, and out of one-half pound they coin 28 *tostoes*, which are worth 100 *reais* each. But who pays for the expenditures and how much these amount to, I do not know, as I live far away from there. This increase in the value of money in that kingdom contributed in no small measure to large amounts being paid for the coins of 1,500 *reais*, and to the quick spoliation of the kingdom, and to the disappearance of the great amount of them that were available in other times. They tell me that the merchants from here in Castile brought huge amounts, and that they sold each coin of 1,000 *reais* for 33 silver *reales*, which taken to Portugal were worth 1,320 *reais*. That is why I warned King Sebastian that it would be convenient to increase the price of gold, and such is what I taught as professor. But it was useless, and even today the *tostoes*, both the old as well as the new ones of little weight, are exchanged for the same price of 100 *reais*, which makes them slowly disappear, either because they are taken abroad, or because they are given to goldsmiths in order to turn them to silver ingots that are sold for a much higher price than the one they have today in Portugal. Likewise, there are many today who also exchange those gold coins, even if they are scarce today, for the price of 1,000 *reais*, or at least exchanged them up to the day when I left that kingdom.

Here I want to give one word of caution. Even if the value of gold or silver coins were to increase or diminish, the copper coin, called a *real* in Portugal, maintains the same value when it is a question of paying amounts of *aúreos* or other coins that were owed, or taxes or penalties enforced by the law, as we saw in argument 312. But they do not have the same value if it is a question of exchanging them in different places, according to the merchants' usual practice, which even today is their custom, since for 10 *reales* that are worth 400 *reais* in Portugal, 11 *reales* are not paid in Castile even if they are worth in Castile 374 *maravedis*, but only 10 *reales* are paid, exchanging them on equal terms and setting aside for the time being the increase in price due to exchange. This is because in these exchanges more importance is given to the amount of silver comparing it to an equal amount of silver, or to the amount of gold comparing it to an equal amount of gold of the same purity, than to the amount of copper and its price in different places. That is why, when the Portuguese silver *real* was worth 36²⁄₇ *reais*, the Castilian *maravedi* was worth more than the Portuguese copper *real* among the merchants, at the rate in which 36²⁄₇ *reais* exceed 34 *maravedis*. And for the same reason, silver *real* and silver *real* were exchanged as equal coins from Portugal to Castile and vice versa, and they exchanged a *ducat* for a *ducat* also as equal coins, even if the *ducat* was worth 400 *reais* in Portugal and 375 *maravedis* in Castile. Therefore, because the value of the silver *real* rose in Portugal to 40 *reais*, the Portuguese copper *real* is worth today less than a *maravedi* at the rate in which 40 *reais* exceed 34 *maravedis*. Therefore, when the value of the silver *real* rose they were exchanged as equal coins from Portugal to Castile and vice versa, and the *ducats* were also exchanged as equal, even if it was worth 400 *reais* in Portugal and 375 *maravedis* in Castile. This explains why, since the value of the silver *real* rose in Portugal to 40 *reais*, the Portuguese copper *real* is worth today less than the *maravedis* at the rate in which 40 *reais* exceed 34 *maravedis*. That is why, when the value of the silver *real* rose to 40 *reais* and the weight of the Portuguese silver *tostón* diminished, the value of the Portuguese copper *real* diminished, in such a way that comparing it to the same copper coin, the value of those Portuguese coins rose among the merchants, just as it increased when buying goods with them. The law becomes ridiculous when it fails to increase the extra charge of these coins in comparison to a same copper coin, because one has to be a fool to hand over today in Portugal a coin of 27½ silver *reales* for 25 *reales* just because in Portugal the price of the silver *real* has risen to 40 *reais*, especially since that same coin is worth much more if it is brought back to Castile or to any other nation, and since more goods are not bought today with 40 *reais* than before with 36, as prices of all goods have risen in Portugal in a continuous way with regard to that copper coin. On account of this, when the silver *real* rose to 40 *reais*, the value of the gold coins started rightfully rising in an incessant way regarding the same copper coins. So it may be understood that a 22⅛-carat gold half pound is worth today in Portugal much more than 30,000 *reais*, at the rate in which 40 *reais* exceed those 36²⁄₇.

I have said all these things about the price of silver coins in Portugal in order to understand and explain all this. I hope they shed sufficient light on what I will say about exchanges.

The mass of gold does not have a price fixed by the law in Castile and Portugal, nor does the mass of silver, except for the fact that in Castile the mass of 11 *denari* and 4 grains may not be sold at more than 65 *reales* for the half pound. But it is not forbidden to buy it for less, and every day they buy and sell for lower prices, each one for what he can obtain. It is easy, thus, to answer the question of whether or not the following silver purchase is just or unjust and if there is or is not an obligation to restitute.

Many people, in great need of money, sell the artistic silver objects they have, and when they offer them for sale to artisans and merchants they do not get a better price than if the silver were not carved, even if the artistic work is at times of great value. Moreover, there are times when they do not receive for the silver more than 64 *reales* for the half pound, so that, aside from the artistic value, they have to reduce even one more *real* per half pound in the silver's value. The question is whether or not such purchase is unfair, and if there is obligation to restitute. I believe that the answer should be this: Since no human law is broken and the artisans and merchants invest in this material great money so that, once the silver has been purified and adapted, they can resell it for more money, the transaction may not be condemned as unjust as long as, given all the circumstances and in the wise men's opinion, they do not go beyond the lowest just price. Keep in mind that this is the artisans' manner of buying because of their activity, such as the booksellers buy the books they receive cheaply in order to sell them more expensively at a later date and, likewise, the merchandise offered unexpectedly is worth less. However, it may happen that the artistic value of the object is so great and so great the hope of being able to resell it in a short time for a much higher price, that the purchase may be considered unjust at times, having to restitute the difference until the lowest just price is reached, even if the half pound is paid at 65 *reales*, and regardless of the fact that in these cases the price is not indivisible but allows for a wide range between the maximum and the minimum just price. And one should not condemn the practices accepted by custom, as custom is a great influence for the price in this type of purchase, which is not to be judged unjust.

Sometimes, those who sell these kinds of objects make a deal with those who buy them wherein they do not resell them for a certain time, so that they are able to recover them within that period of time for a certain amount and a higher one than the one they now receive. Some are skeptical regarding the justness of this contract, suspecting that it conceals usury. I believe that the following should be the response. In order for that contract to be licit and just, one should abide by the following conditions: (1) the first sale should be a genuine sale, so that if during the time when the buyer is awaiting payment the object perishes, it perishes for the buyer; (2) the first sale should be just, according to what we have said; (3) a price higher than the price that the first buyer, present owner of the object, could obtain from any other buyer should not be fixed for the second sale when the object is recovered. These conditions prevent the contract from being usurious or unjust and make it a gratuitous contribution of the first buyer to the one who first sold the object, promising not to resell it to a third party for a certain period of time. We described this in argument 376 and gave some examples to make it clear.

Finally, what we have explained in this argument shall help us to better understand the following. In olden times, in this kingdom of Castile there were *ducats* worth 375 *maravedis* and, in Portugal, those same *ducats* or *cruzados* were worth 400 *reais*, and money was taken from one place to another to carry out the contracts. In many contracts they mentioned the *ducats*, not only in these kingdoms, but also in the affairs with other provinces, and even today they celebrate exchanges and other types of contracts where they order many things in terms of the *ducat* as standard. However, there has not been in these kingdoms for a long time a coin that is worth what a *ducat* is worth, so that the value of what in other times was understood as a *ducat*, and today is still understood, is paid by compensating with an equal sum of money in other coins. Such is the evidence of everyday custom.

Argument 401

Whether a Higher Price Than the One Set by the Law May Licitly Be Received for the Coins to Which the Public Authority Assigned a Particular Value at the Moment of Coinage

What was analyzed in the previous argument shall illustrate what we now go on to say. Pay heed to the existence of a custom, accepted in some provinces such as Flanders and Italy, by which the common price set by the law is not considered so rigid that it may not fluctuate according to the greater or lesser abundance of coins or the amount of people who desire them, as happens with the price of goods that are not appraised by the law. Thus, for example, they tell me that in Rome, even if the common value of the gold *escudo* is 12½ *julios*, that value suddenly increases in copper coins, even twice a month, diminishing later. And the more or less abundance of these copper coins depends on the scarcity or demand of the *escudos*, as well as on other circumstances. Wherever this custom exists, there is no doubt that it shall be licit to receive this extra charge. The difficulty seems to present itself in those places where the price of currency is set by the public authority by law in order to keep it unalterable, such as happened in the Spanish territories and in other provinces, where they used to appraise their own coins.

However, even in that case it must be said that for reason of profit ceasing, sometimes it is licit to receive something more than the legal price for the coins, taking into account the estimation of that profit's amount. For example, if a person had set money apart to take to another place where it was worth more, or to use it to buy merchandise in a place where the coins of his place of residency could not be bought, or only by losing a part of their value, this person may, when exchanging his coins for others, collect the amount in which he estimates the profit ceasing. This is the opinion of Juan de Medina,[1] among others.

At the end of argument 364, in a similar case, we said that the owner of a lot of wheat the price of which is appraised by the law, could receive for reason of profit ceasing something more than that price if he were planning to take it to a place where it was worth more. However, he had to avoid creating a scandal. For the same reason, if an artisan, who had prepared the coins that he was going to use to cover with gold the objects he produces, were to lend them to someone who asks insistently for them, making him lose the benefit he hoped to obtain from his work as an artisan, he may receive in turn, together with the common price of the coins, the amount he estimates is the profit of which he is truly being deprived.

In Portugal it is forbidden to destroy silver coins or send them to be destroyed, even if they are coins from another kingdom, in order to produce artistic objects with them, or for any other reason. There is also a penalty of a ten-year banishment to someplace in Africa, together with the loss of half the goods, which shall be divided between the informer and the royal tax authorities.[2] Under the same penalties it is forbidden to choose the heavier coins and sell them later according to their weight. Whoever did any of these things, if he were a minister of the king, in charge of receiving his money, would bring upon himself

1. Juan de Medina, *De cambiis* (Salamanca, 1550), q. 3, § antepenúlt.

2. *Ordenações Manuelinas*, lib. 5, tit. 6, § últ.

the death penalty and loss of all his goods. I do not know if such rigorous law is actually applied, making us judge the artisan or private person who destroys a few silver coins to produce an artistic object as guilty of mortal sin, especially, after the silver *real* has risen until reaching a price of 40 *reais*, and the weight of the *tostón* has diminished, as we said in the previous argument. For if such law were upheld with all its force and continued being applied because the circumstances are the same as when it was promulgated, there would be no doubt that it compels under mortal sin, because of the gravity of the offense and the harm that follows for the republic. For, as experience proves, it is the heavier coins and of a same value that are destroyed. However, this law does not deal with the silver coins that have no value in Portugal, as the laws clearly state.[3]

In the kingdom of Castile it is also prohibited under death penalty and loss of all goods to destroy gold, silver, or copper coins, or carry them out of the kingdom.[4] But I understand that this law, promulgated by the Catholic Kings,[5] does not apply to the old coins that are today rare and were followed by others, when it is those that are destroyed in order to gild some objects, since this is something insignificant and the change in times and circumstances make it licit.

Although the exchange of coins in one and the same place should be carried out for an equal value, if there were grounds to fear that over a short period of time a coin was going to be devaluated by public authority, it could be bought licitly for a lower price than the legal one, as such fear and the probability

3. *Leis extravagantes*, part. 4, tit. 11, law 3, § 3–9.

4. N. R. 5.21.67 (Ed. note: Cf. N. N. R. 12.8.3); N. R. 8.17.6 (Ed. note: Cf. N. N. R. 18.8.2).

5. Ed. note: The title "Catholic King" or "Catholic Kings" refers in the singular either to Ferdinand II of Aragón (1452–1516), son of John II of Aragón and Johanna Enríquez or, in the plural, to Ferdinand II of Aragón and Isabella (1451–1504), daughter of John II of Castile and Isabella of Portugal.

of devaluation make it lose value just as money that is at risk of a storm, or of other dangers at sea, is justly bought for a lower price than the one appraised by law. Such is Medina's opinion in the last paragraph of the place cited earlier. But while those coins are not devaluated by public authority, they may be licitly handed over at the appraised price, because in truth, they still maintain their old value, as they may be given and spent for the same uses in which they would be spent if there did not exist any fear of their devaluation.

In the already cited argument,[6] Medina ascertains that while the law that appraises a coin is still in force, it is not licit to receive for said coins a price that is higher than the one appraised, even if the metal of which they are made has many other applications—for example, if it were gold of many carats (as usually happens with old coins) and were better for gilding objects, ornamentation, health reasons, and similar things. Medina's reason is that when a coin is appraised, they take into account the purity of the metal and the possible uses of it, and once all things are pondered, they fix the value of the metal to which a seal is applied, making it a coin. Therefore, just as with wheat it is not licit to receive a greater price than that appraised by law because the legal price is indivisible; it is not licit either in the case of coins to receive a greater price to that which is legal. And if it were received, there is obligation to restitute.

But Medina adds: If it became a custom to receive for certain coins something more than the price appraised by law, and the prince or senate knew about it and did not punish or tried to prevent it, one should consider that it is the prince's will that the law not be applied in this point, because of which such increment over the legal price may be accepted without fear. I would go on to add that, from then on, such extra charge falls within the limits of the just natural price, which is not rigid or indivisible, as would be the legal price. And this is why Medina considers the

6. Medina, *De cambiis*, q. 3, § antepenúlt.

practice of receiving an extra charge for certain old, gold coins is something that is free of blame and the obligation to restitute.

According to this opinion, we shall have to decide if the first ones who started receiving that increment, before the tacit and presumed consent of the prince, did sin, and have the obligation to give back to those from whom they received it, as the law was still in force.

Soto, Navarrus, Covarrubias, Silvestre, and Cajetan acknowledge that a coin may be considered under two aspects:[7] one, as coin; the other, as metal, that is, as gold of a greater or lesser purity, greater or lesser weight. And they say that if, given all circumstances, it had a certain value as metal, it would be licit to receive a higher price than that set by the law, as the price set by the law refers to the coins as such, that is, as price to pay for purchases, even if when assigning that value they had taken into account the value of the material it is made of and its possible applications. Many add that no one may be forced to give for a coin a price that is above that established by the law, nor to receive it as if it had a lower value than the legal one, because of which it shall be licit to buy them at their legal price and sell them later for a higher price.

Regarding this issue, I shall briefly state my opinion. One word of caution before anything else is to say that when coins are minted and a price is fixed on them, the material they are made of is never worth more, even if all possible applications are taken into account, than the price fixed on them. Furthermore, it does not even reach the price, as the minting expenses

7. Domingo de Soto, *De iustitia et iure, libri decem* (Salamanca, 1553), lib. 6, q. 9; Martín de Azpilcueta, *Manual de confesores y penitentes* (Salamanca, 1556), cap. 17, no. 288; Martín de Azpilcueta, *Comentario resolutorio de usuras* (Salamanca, 1556), cap. últ., no. 20; Diego de Covarrubias y Leyva, *De collatione veterum nummismatum* (Venice, 1581), cap. 7, no. 3, in princ.; Silvestre de Prierias, *Sylvestrina summa, qua summa summarum merito nuncupatur* (Lyons, 1555), verb. usura, 4, q. 3; Tomás de Vio Cajetan, *De cambiis* (Milan, 1499), cap. 6.

and, in this case, the tribute paid to the prince are deducted from the metal with which the coins are minted. It would be foolish for a prince who is ordered to mint a coin to fix on it an inferior price to the value of the metal it is made of. The price is fixed taking into account the abundance of a certain metal at the time, its possible applications and all other circumstances, making it improbable to find a better price for that metal. What Medina says about this is true. We should also add that for the mere fact of minting a gold coin that is inferior in carats or in weight, and fixing an equal or even higher price to that of the coins that have been on hand up to then, it should be assumed that the law that had fixed the price of the preceding coins ceases to be in force, and that everyone may increase the price of these preceding coins within the limits of what is naturally just. Justice asks that, all things considered, things of an equal value have an equal price, unless the prince was to order the contrary for a reasonable cause. And it would be irrational and unjust that he order it without reasonable cause, since fixing unequal prices to goods of equal value without reasonable cause is irrational and injurious to his subjects.

The laws of Castile and Portugal are in agreement with this doctrine of ours, clearly and manifestly. Thus, for example, when Philip appraised the *escudos* so that from then on they would be worth 400 *maravedis*[8] and ordered that for no reason at all could anyone receive a higher price for them, he equally declared that the ducats that Ferdinand and Isabella had ordered to be minted out of finer gold had a greater value than when they had been minted, due to the greater weight and greater quantity of gold in them. This is the reason why he ordered they be worth 429 *maravedis*, as we explained in the preceding argument. And it is undeniable that before the rise in the price of the *escudos*, nobody could justly condemn receiving a proportionate price

8. N. R. 5.21.13.

for the *ducats*, in view of not only the greater weight, but also the greater quantity of highly pure gold that they contained.

In Portugal, the law similarly explains the greater value of the grain of gold of the 24-carat *cruzados* over the value of the grain of gold of 22⅛-carat coins, explaining that the grain of gold of these last coins is worth 6½ *reais*, while the value of the grain of gold of the first coins was of 7 *reais* plus one-third of a *septil*.[9] And in this way it goes on to explain the value of the grain in intermediate coins.

In the third place, it is important to point out that when gold coins are minted and a price is fixed on them, there is usually an abundance of that kind of gold, and the price is fixed according to this abundance, taking into account all existing circumstances. But if the circumstances were to change with time, and having carried those highly pure gold coins out of the kingdom, whether to be used for gilding or for decorating objects, the value of the metal of such coins increased considerably, it should not be assumed that the legislators would want the laws that fixed the old rates to still be in force. And even if they wanted to, it would neither be just nor fair, because they may be sold for their natural just price not only as goods but as price with which they pay for all other things, without there being any sin or obligation to restitute, because, as Medina rightly believes, the coin's purpose is always the same, under whatever form it is considered. In the case described, good public ministers do not oppose or punish those who proceed in the way described, nor do they use their power to persecute their subjects harshly and unjustly, but they apply the interpretation of the laws according to the circumstances of time, place, thing, and people and understand that such laws can no longer be applied, as the present circumstances are very different from those in which the laws were issued. Consequently, even if the laws of Ferdinand and Isabella are included in the mentioned section 21, book 5

9. *Leis extravagantes*, part. 4, tit. 11, law 4, § 3–9.

of the *Nueva Recopilación*, because a great part of its content is still in force, it does not apply when it comes to the rate of the *ducat*'s value, as King Philip himself declared in law 13 cited earlier. Even before this declaration it had already ceased to be in force, as we have indicated. Nor are the words used to order obeying those rates in force. King Philip ordered that for no reason should a higher price than the one he himself appraised be received for the *escudos*, because when this law was issued there was, as even today there is, a great abundance of *escudos*. But when it was time to deal with the old *ducats*, he only defined the value they have today, taking into account the value that has been given to them without adding those words that say that for no reason should it be licit to receive for them a greater price, because, given their scarcity, the need for them and their utility for some things, it would be licit to receive for them their whole natural value, presuming those circumstances exist. In brief, it is licit to receive for any coin what would licitly be received for a piece of gold of the same weight and purity at any time, as the amount of gold in the coin is not of a worse quality for being converted into coin than if it were not. On the contrary, it is of better condition and greater value on account of the fact that one may receive for it something more than what is received for an equal piece of gold.

From what is declared here and was declared earlier in the preceding argument, it shall be easy to understand that the Portuguese laws that appraised the price of gold coins do not in all conscience force anyone today, because of which a greater price may be received for those worsened coins, even if it should always be done within the limits of their natural value. And the same should be said about the more impure gold coins that were appraised 1,000 or 500 *reais*, as the law that appraised the silver *real* lost its legal force for the very fact that the silver *real* increased its value up to 40 *reais*. Also, for that same reason there were no longer any scruples nor difficulties over receiving a greater price for them than the one rated by the law when they were to be carried somewhere else, as today nobody offers for them more than 40 *reais*.

Both in Castile as well as in Portugal, the laws have established today how much the price of old gold coins has risen, and how much they are worth today. Therefore, if someone wanted to pay his creditor with these coins, the creditor would be forced to receive them at the price fixed by the law and, in all fairness, would not be able to receive them as if they had a lower price, as the price fixed by the law is the lowest just price they have today, and there is no one who hands them over for a lower price, unless they ignore their value. In regard to the greater price some coins are exchanged for today, it may be taken in all fairness, even if it exceeds the legal price. This is what we said about the Portuguese coins worth 1,500 *reais*. But a creditor may not be forced to take them for that higher price, since the extra charge given for them does not affect the legal price but the natural one, and there are many who hand over those coins for the price fixed on them by the law in other times. And as long as nothing else is ordered or declared, one should judge that that price does not go beyond the limits of the lowest just price. It is the debtor who may choose to find someone who gives him a higher price for them, and then make the payment in other currencies.

Argument 402

If an Employee Who Was Taking Money in Gold Coins to Pay Some Debts, or to Make Some Purchases, Took Advantage on the Way of an Opportunity Offered to Exchange Those Coins for a Better Price, Could That Employee Appropriate for Himself the Extra Charge Obtained in This Manner?

The matter we are discussing in this argument happened frequently in Portugal when I was teaching these subjects. At the time there was an abundance of coins (1,500 *reais*) and debts were paid with them, or they were handed over to an envoy to be used to buy merchandise for their owners. According to what we have said, it was possible to exchange the coins with an additional benefit over the price they had been appraised for when minted, without breaking the law for it. The issue in question is whether the envoy under discussion, when knowing beforehand who was willing to give that extra charge, or looking for that person himself, might carry out that exchange and get for himself the extra charge using the rest of the money to pay the debt or buy the merchandise as they had ordered him to do. May he keep the extra charge or should he restitute it? And who does he owe the restitution to?

The same uncertainty exists regarding the officers of the king who are in charge of collecting the royal revenue, and other ministers who carry out similar duties for other members of the aristocracy and, in general, the depositaries to whom many debts are paid in currency that they have no obligation of assessing for a higher price, and then, by order of the king, or of whomever they are ministers, who pay salaries, debts, and other expenses. During the time between the collection and the payment, these people have the opportunity to exchange the collected coins for other coins, thus obtaining an increment, and it is uncertain whether they may keep that extra charge or should restitute it.

I believe the doubts regarding this issue shall be explained with the following conclusions: First, in all of the above cases, if after exchanging the gold coins with an extra charge, the officer or depositary buys other gold coins that are similar to those initially received and with them carries out the commission for the one who ordered him to do so, he may certainly keep the extra charge as the fruits of his ingenuity, even if for obtaining it he may have taken someone else's money as an instrument to do so. It is clear because by doing so he did no harm, either by hurting the person in whose name he negotiated or the person to whom he had to hand over the money, due to the fact that, as we are to assume, he gave this person in due time coins of the same type and the same value as those that had been handed over to him, which makes it evident that he carried out the commission he received, allowing him to keep the profit that the extra charge stands for. This is substantiated by what shall be said in the third conclusion.

If the owner's usual wish were that the debt be paid in the same currency as that which he handed over, because he favored the payee's own good to that of the envoy's, and the payee wanted to employ it in lesser expenses with an equal or greater benefit in the exchange, the envoy shall be forced to restitute the payee of all the profit he was deprived of, unless he delivers coins of the same quality as those received. It is clear because against the will of both the payer and the payee, the payee is denied the just benefit that he was going to collect with the coin exchange, because of which there is offense and he should receive restitution.

It could happen that the payee did not intend to obtain any special benefit from the coins because, for example, he was thinking of spending them, handing them over for their usual lowest price, and that the owner of the coins regularly favored the envoy's own good to that of the payee's, or did not even bother about it. In that case, I believe the envoy would be able to keep that profit, and it would not be an impediment that the sender wanted that profit for himself rather than for the employee.

To prove this conclusion, it is necessary to go over what was said in argument 327: What the usurer, thief, or payee gain when they negotiate with something that is not theirs is consumable by use and they have acquired it for themselves through usury, theft, or receipt as deposit, and so they are forced to restitute only those things they received that belonged to someone else, or other equivalent things, as well as the profit ceasing that the owners could have endured because of the delay in restitution. From this we can establish the following argument to prove the first part of the conclusion: In the case set forth, the profit does not belong to the sender nor to the payee more than what it would had the envoy stolen the money or extorted money from them through usury. Therefore, just as neither the thief nor the usurer have the obligation to hand over the profit obtained, and they only have to pay up what they took (as we clearly proved in the above cited argument), neither shall the envoy in our case be forced to restitute that profit, except only to give back what he took. In truth, this is what he does when he gives the payee the money for what it would be worth in his hands. We may also use the following argument: If the envoy had not obtained any profit with the money but had lost it gambling or spent it buying goods for their lowest price (as was sometimes done), and if the payee was going to spend the money with a better exchange, it is certain that no confessor would force him to restitute any part except that which would have been spent in that better way. In our case, the envoy should also not be forced to make further restitution.

The following objection may be raised: Such profit obtained by the thief, usurer, or envoy proceeds from something that belongs to someone else, and only from the value it has when the thief, usurer, or envoy take hold of it. Consequently, it does not belong to these, but to the owner of the money or to his payee as the fruit of something that belongs to them, and not of the ingenuity of the one who carried out the exchange, even if neither the sender nor the payee had the intention of collecting that gain. So we see that the fruits from a farm or from a horse belong to the owner of the farm or horse even if the owner had not collected them.

To this argument I respond by allowing the antecedent but refuting the consequent. For even if such profit comes from the thing itself and its value, it is not, however, the fruit of it but of the ingenuity of the person who negotiates with it and the person who buys with it to his own advantage or disadvantage, and if by giving it such use it should perish, it does not because of this perish for its owner, who has to receive full payment. And the one who negotiates with the profit without owning it shall have to account for it in case there is a judicial complaint. The fruits of the thing—for example, of the horse or the farm—are not the thing itself and its value, but the fruit of them or of the use that has been made of them; or they are the price received for those fruits, which is a subsequent fruit to the thing received—for example, for the use of the horse or for the apples produced by the farm. Now then, what is earned by negotiating with a good at the risk of only the person who negotiates with it is fruit of his ingenuity and, thus, the profit we refer to belongs to the envoy who, at his own risk and for his own benefit, exchanged the coins.

I shall go on to prove the second part of the conclusion, that is, that in case the sender is usually satisfied that the profit from the exchange is greater for the envoy than for the payee (or simply did not bother about it), the envoy could licitly keep said profit, even in the case in which the payee could have obtained a greater profit in the transaction. This is because the money sent—either as donation, payment for a debt, or in exchange for something else—does not belong to the payee until he accepts it. Until said moment of acceptance it belongs to the sender, who may revoke the donation or the order (as was said countless times in argument 263 and others). Consequently, everything the sender or the envoy does with the money, before the acceptance happens on the payee's part and according to the owner's presumed decision that at least it is not something he finds objectionable, is not injurious to the payee and does not require compensation for depriving him of the profit that through the coin exchange he wished to obtain. However, if the one transporting the money is a servant of the payee or someone who accepted the money following his orders and received it in his name, then, because the payee acquired the property by accepting the money (according to what was said in the above mentioned argument and in several others) by depriving him now of the profit obtained for the exchange, the envoy is wronging him and must compensate for everything he is being deprived of collecting, even if the envoy had obtained with his transactions a smaller profit or no profit at all.

The third part of the conclusion said that it made no difference that the sender preferred the profit for himself rather than for the envoy. It is clear, because if the envoy had stolen the money under discussion from the sender, the subsequent profit would not belong to the owner of the money, notwithstanding his desire for such profit to go to him instead of to the thief, who would not be compelled to compensate but for the losses, including the profit ceasing. Consequently, in our case, the profit does not belong to the owner of the money either but to the employee, notwithstanding the master's contrary disposition to it.

It should be pointed out that sometimes the property of a deposit does not belong to the depositor but to the depositary, who receives it at his own risk, without being compelled to return the same deposit in numeric terms. Such is the case of the public money depositaries and recipients, whom they call *almojarifes*[1] or *tesoreros*[2] of the king, and others of the like. Consequently, what we said is even truer, as even if they receive gold coins at the current price, they fulfill their obligations by giving back its value in any other currency and by paying the king—or his ministers or anyone else by his command—in any currency. And if they make any profit by exchanging the coins, theirs shall be the profit, as this is one of the advantages they obtain in the form of salary for their occupation.

1. Ed. note: *almojarifes*: storekeepers.
2. Ed. note: *tesoreros*: treasurers.

Argument 403

On the Usefulness of Exchanging Money from One Place to Another

On the Type of Exchange in Which the Banker Receives the Money in Advance

We have explained up to here what petty exchange is. Let us now discuss the exchange from one place to another, that is, by means of bills of exchange. This type of exchange is useful and even necessary for many reasons because often there is someone who needs in one place money that he has in another place, whether to bring merchandise from there to where he needs it, or to live there or for any other expense. However, he cannot take that money there either because it is forbidden to carry it out of the kingdom or because it may not be carried by sea without great danger and with due speed, because of thieves or other similar causes, and without incurring great expense, effort, and inconveniences. And even if none of these circumstances were true, the money under discussion may not be worth anything in the place where he needs it or worth as much as in the place in which he has it. For these and other reasons, men find it useful to exchange money in one place for money they have available in another, for their own good or the common good. We would like to examine now whether or not bankers may licitly charge an increment and obtain a profit for this exchange of money when taking it from one place to another.

Money may have in different places a different value for several causes, and it is necessary to ponder how much the exchange should increase or decrease because of the difference in value in order to make the contract licit and just. Therefore, we must first of all examine whether or not in the case when the money has the same value in both places the banker may collect an increase because of the formal or virtual transportation he carries out for the sake of the person seeking the exchange. This type of exchange may be carried out in two ways: First, when the banker receives the money first to hand it back later in a different place personally or through his correspondent. In this case, it does not seem to be a loan nor, for this reason, usury on the banker's part. An example may be someone who is considering going to Rome and gives the banker 100 here so that when he gets to Rome the banker or his correspondent in the city should give him 90. The other way would be if the banker first gives the money to receive it himself or through a correspondent in another place with an increment, and here it does appear there is a combination of a loan on the banker's part. The doctors' opinion of each of these cases is different, and we shall discuss the first case in this argument, leaving the second for the following one.

All doctors agree that it is licit to charge an increment for the exchange carried out in the first case, as long as, in the prudent people's opinion, it does not exceed the value of the formal or virtual transportation of the money from one place to another, taking into account the distance, dangers, and the rest of the circumstances.[1] King Sebastian did not forbid these types of

1. Conrado de Summenhart, *Opus septipartitum de contractibus* (Hannover, 1500), q. 99, concl. 4 and 11, reg. 3; concl. 12, corol. 3, 5, and others, especially 12; Juan de Medina, *De cambiis* (Salamanca, 1550), q. 4; Domingo de Soto, *De iustitia et iure, libri decem* (Salamanca, 1553), lib. 6, q. 10, art. 1; Tomás de Vio Cajetan, *De cambiis* (Milan, 1499), caps. 1 and 6; Martín de Azpilcueta, *Manual de confesores y penitentes* (Salamanca, 1556), cap. 17, no. 289; Azpilcueta, *Comentario resolutorio de usuras* (Salamanca, 1556), cap. final, no. 21; Gabriel Biel, *Commentarii doctissimi in IV sententiarum*

exchanges in the law he promulgated in 1570. What is more, he ratified them, as is clear to whoever reads said law. Pius V is of the same opinion in the bull he published on exchanges.

The reason for accepting it is the following: The transportation of the money for the sake of the one who solicits the exchange warrants a price, since the muleteer and navigator licitly charge payment for transporting money from one place to another. And they charge more the greater the distance, the greater the dangers on the road, the greater the amount of money, and so on regarding other circumstances, which may increase the value of transportation. So, too, the banker licitly receives the stipend that corresponds to the transportation he is carrying out. And it is beside the point that, in general, the banker is not the one carrying out a formal or real transportation because in faraway places he has employees or correspondents who carry out the payment of the money, because, as the doctors are right in pointing out, the person who solicits the exchange for a certain place is rendered the same service as if the bankers themselves were truly transporting the coins there. And the fact that they can do this easier than others and with minimum expense and no danger and almost no effort is due to their cleverness and organization, and is not an impediment for them to be able to charge a proportionate stipend for the services rendered. Notice, however, that the means they have in many places to bring or take sums of money at the service of not one but many people, and the possibility of dedicating themselves at the same time to other lucrative businesses, decreases the value of the transportation under discussion, and the banker may not in justice charge each one as if he actually took the coins of one and not of many. The just price of this exchange, if not appraised by the law—and it usually is not—cannot be established with absolute precision

libros (Brescia, 1574), dist. 15, q. 11, art. 3, dub. 12; John Major, *In quartum sententiarum quaestiones utilissimae* (Paris, 1521), q. 37; *Ordenações Manuelinas*, lib. 4, tit. 14, § 5.

but fluctuates within certain limits that a prudent person should establish, in much the same way that we said in argument 348 that the limits of the natural just price should be set. In order to judge whether a price is right in these matters, it helps to know what is regularly charged, as long as more than what the circumstances call for is not charged through the tyranny of a monopoly or for the insatiable thirst of increasing the price of things. It is evident that the amount of those soliciting the exchange and the scarcity of bankers increase the price of this exchange, as, on the contrary, the amount of bankers and scarcity of those who solicit the exchange decrease it. It is the same as with everything: the multitude of buyers and the scarcity of sellers make prices rise and, conversely, the multitude of sellers and the scarcity of buyers makes them fall. Medina, Navarrus, and Major have already observed this in the places to which we already referred regarding the price of exchanges, even if Medina appears not to have understood the reason regarding virtual transportation.

In the type of exchange discussed in this and the following argument there is a combination of two contracts: one, the exchange of one coin for another, which should be carried out respecting the equality; the other, the rental of services and the necessary activity to transport the money from one place to another, at least virtually. Because of this last endeavor, a stipend may be received. Both in the money exchange and in the payment of the increment for the service rendered or which shall be rendered, there is a transfer of property.

In the exchange we are referring to in the present argument there may be injustice on the banker's part, and there shall be obligation to restitute if he were to charge a greater increment than what was warranted for the services rendered. But there cannot be usury, as the banker does not formally or virtually grant a loan. But whoever signs with him an exchange contract does virtually grant the banker a loan, as he first gives him the money in one place so that it is returned somewhere else. The person who grants it may commit usury, because of which he would be forced to restitute. This is the case, for example, if he realizes that the banker needs the money here and he gives it to the banker so that the banker gives him back the same amount in a distant place. In that case, he would be asking the banker for something in addition to the capital—namely, the effort of transporting the money to a distant place, and this deserves payment. Thus, he commits usury and has to restitute the amount in which the transportation is estimated. So say Navarrus and others in the places before cited. He would have the obligation of a much greater restitution if he stipulates that the banker give him an equal sum of money in a place which, for the reason we shall shortly explain, the money shall be worth more. For, in such case, he would virtually receive a much greater increment for the money he gave in advance. But if the money had the same value in one and the other place, and the distance between them were not great, it could be presumed that the banker turns the increment down out of generosity, or as a reward for other favors, due to the fact that the stipend for transportation would be small. But if the stipend were significant, there would need to be sufficient reasons to persuade oneself in good conscience that the banker absolves him from his payment. And if two people needed to transport money, for example, one from Lisbon to Toledo and the other from Toledo to Lisbon, even if one of them is a banker and the other is not, it would be licit to hand over the money in one place in order for the other person to hand back the same amount in the other place. For, as we shall see in the two following arguments, either one of them can licitly sell the virtual transportation of the money that the other needs, and there would even be more sense in licitly compensating each other for the respective transportations.

Argument 404

On Whether It Is Licit for the Banker to Charge a Certain Increment for the Exchange He Gives When He Anticipates the Money in One Place to Recover It in a Different Place

Some experts considered this type of exchange to be illicit and usurious, and forced the person to restitute the increment thus received. They justified their opinion saying it does not seem that the banker transports any money, which would be the reason why he could licitly receive said increment due to the services he rendered by transporting it, and there does not seem to be any other reason for that increment other than waiting for future payment, making it a formal or virtual loan, and therefore usurious, as the increment thus received is considered such. This opinion is defended in the Portuguese ordinances[1] when they condemn this contract as usurious and consider the banker who acts in this way liable to the penalties established against the usurers.

However, the contrary opinion seems more usual among the doctors, that is, that said contract of exchange shall not be usurious as long as the increment is not received for reason of the delay in payment but for the service and virtual transportation of the money. So say Conrado, Cajetan, Soto, Navarrus,

1. *Ordenações Manuelinas*, lib. 4, tit. 14, § 6.

Juan de Medina, and others.[2] King Sebastian's law promulgated November 5, 1577, agrees with this opinion, in which law four fairs or markets that were never celebrated were conceded to Portugal. That law authorizes, not only in fairs, but at other times, receiving money in exchange in Seville to pay it back with a certain increment in Portugal. In his bull on exchanges, Pius V not only does not reject this opinion, but explicitly approves it.

This opinion may be proved by observing that the money that is given in a faraway place is not worth so much that its delivery there may be compensated with the same goods that would be delivered here for that money if it had any value here. For as faraway money it is coupled to the transportation that with effort and expense shall carry out the person who must make the payment, there being a just price for this transportation. Thus, when the banker anticipates the money in one place and agrees to receive the payment in another place, if the person who receives the money is released from the effort and expense involved in transporting the money he has elsewhere in order to compensate with that money the amount he receives here, then the exchange dealer may receive a just price for the transportation he provides in the same amount that another exchange dealer would receive from this same person. This is so that the money the exchange dealer gave him in the place where the person is may be paid in the faraway place referred to in the contract with the first exchange dealer. And it is beside the point if this exchange dealer has a representative in the place where the money is, allowing him to carry out the money transference without any effort or expense, as this is something that happens

2. Conrado de Summenhart, *Opus septipartitum de contractibus* (Hannover, 1500), q. 99; Tomás de Vio Cajetan, *De cambiis* (Milan, 1499), cap. 6; Domingo de Soto, *De iustitia et iure, libri decem* (Salamanca, 1553), lib. 6, q. 10, art. 1; Martín de Azpilcueta, *Manual de confesores y penitentes* (Salamanca, 1556), cap. 17, nos. 289, 290, 294; Azpilcueta, *Comentario resolutorio de usuras* (Salamanca, 1556), cap. final, no. 25; Juan de Medina, *De cambiis* (Salamanca, 1550), qq. 4 and 5.

per accidens, due to his fortunate situation. This service may be assessed in monetary terms.

This is the reason Cajetan identifies in the place already cited, and Navarrus considers more extensively in the cited *Comentario*, numbers 62 and 63, and it is of no consequence if the banker hands over the money before receiving compensation for the money and for releasing the client of the effort of transporting extra money to carry out the payment (as both things should be paid). This is because of the fact that he shall expect payment for both the money he hands over and for releasing the client from the effort of transporting it, which is a favor he does for him, as long as he does not receive anything for waiting to get paid, unless it is because of profit ceasing. This point is proved in the fact that the banker who receives the money here in order to hand over the money that is needed in Rome, for example, to ship some bulls, does not need to be any more industrious and does not incur more expenses than the banker who—with the same end in mind—gives the money in Rome that will be returned to him later on. More so, the service he gives is greater because he gives before receiving. Therefore, what the banker could licitly receive in the first case he may also receive in the second, as he does not receive anything on account of the payment.

Regarding the arguments of those whose opinion is contrary to this one, we should say that the banker under discussion transfers the money, at least virtually or as if it were real, since he releases the person who receives the exchange from the effort of transferring it, as we have already explained, and has been demonstrated with a just argument allowing for the increment. Regarding the Portuguese ordinances, it should be said that even if they consider that the contract we are dealing with here is illicit *ex natura rei*, and makes the banker liable to the established penalties against usurers, this is not so, as we have already proved, because of which the legislators were wrong and such law is not even in force in a court of law. We should add that King Sebastian approved such a contract in the law he later promulgated.

From what has been said, we understand that someone who buys a thing in a faraway place may pay a lower price for it than what it is worth over there when the seller cannot sell it there by retail, if he can bring it without great expense. And this is so even in the case in which the buyer can use it in the place where it is without expense, or can easily sell it by retail in the market for a just price. The reason is that, given the circumstances, the thing is really worth less for the seller who is released from much effort and expense in selling it. All this is extensively explained by Cajetan and Navarrus in the already cited places.[3]

From here I conclude that what the Genovese did in the kingdom of Castile was not something by nature unjust. Many Castilians who lived far away from Seville had annual revenues there that the king owed them for the money he had taken as tribute. When the fleet from the New World arrived in Seville, the Genovese handed over to these people lower annual revenues in the places where they lived, in exchange for the revenue they had in Seville. I do not condemn this exchange of one income for another if the difference that results from the lower payment is moderate, taking into account the burden they released the owners of such tributes from and, also, the great effort it was sometimes to recover from the ministers of the king the sums handed over.

From what has been said I also conclude that there is nothing illicit in doing something I have been often asked about in Lisbon. Many ladies of the Lisbon nobility have annual revenues in Castile, which are given to them ordinarily by the ministers of the king at certain dates. One part of that income is given to a merchant as payment for getting the ministers of the king to pay them the whole amount, receive it, transfer it to Lisbon, and

3. Cajetan, *De cambiis*, cap. 6; Azpilcueta, *Comentario*, cap. final, nos. 62, 63.

give it to them. What is more, some of the ladies allow a present to be offered to the minister of the king, leaving him a share of the owed quantity, so that the payment is not deferred when the merchant shows up to collect the money. In this matter, the king should set clear standards on how the ministers are to proceed, and prevent them from unjustly receiving these gifts and thereby turn these mercenary payments into legitimate settlements. Of course, he should punish them and make them restitute the gifts received. The confessors, in turn, should question these ministers regarding these practices and force them to restitute the gifts that were offered in a not wholly voluntary way to avoid inconveniences to the creditors. On this issue some God-fearing tradesmen were questioned and told me that they went to these same places and there received the money they needed for their commercial dealings, giving it back later in Lisbon from the money they had there. I have told them that the fact that it is useful to them and may be done with scarcely any work is no impediment for them to licitly receive the amount of what it is worth for these ladies to carry out their commercial dealings in such a faraway place and for the virtual transportation of the money. This shall be easier to understand when we explain the following argument.

The stipend they usually receive is the following: They give each lady the entire amount of the gold coins that is theirs (the value of the *ducat* in Portugal is 400 *reais*, while in Castile it is worth 374 *maravedis*), but for each *aúreo* they receive in Castile 11 silver *reales* and, in Portugal, only 10, so that for each *aúreo* or *ducat* they earn 1 silver *real*, which certainly does not seem excessive for collecting the revenues in Castile and taking them back to Portugal, although it is the prudent people who should judge this, and it is always wise to act with moderation in such stipends and profits, especially since these commercial dealings demand little work, scarce effort, and no risk.

Regarding the exchange we are referring to in this argument, in general we should know that nothing is collected for the delay in payment, and because of this, anything that is collected over the rigorous just price that is owed for the other rulings may not be drawn for the delay in collecting, and is usurious and liable to restitution. Because of this it is not more licit to receive it when the payment shall be granted later somewhere else than if the payment is to be granted instantly, or if the money had been previously handed over somewhere else in order to be handed back here later. This was established by Pius V in his bull on exchanges. This, however, should be accepted as long as there is not a real profit ceasing for the delay in payment, as Navarrus[4] says.

Even if Pius V forbids in his bull that the banker fix from the beginning, or whenever, a standard interest rate—even in the case of absence of payment, as Navarrus says when he declared these same words in the number cited—this is based on the hypothesis that it is collected for veiled usury and not for profit ceasing that is a consequence of the delay in payment. For if it were received for a profit that really is ceasing, in the person's conscience it would be licit and just to receive it, and would not be subject to restitution, because the law that is founded on a hypothesis does not apply to the person's conscience when it is evident that the opposite of what is assumed happens to be true.

To prevent any usury from taking place on account of late payments, in the same bull on exchanges Pius V prohibits exchanges made to any but the next fair, if the bills of exchange were signed for a place where these were being celebrated. And if the bills of exchange were signed for a place where a fair was not being celebrated, bills of exchange should not be given but for the nearest fair, according to the custom of allowing changes for that place. Of course, if the next fair were so close in time that it would not be possible for the bills of exchange to arrive on time in order to carry out the payment, then the "next fair" would be considered the following one, as what they are talking about is the next fair in which the payment can be carried out.

4. Azpilcueta, *Manual*, cap. 17, no. 301.

Navarrus, cited in number 301, says when explaining these words that it is not forbidden to arrange the payment for the second, third, or fourth fair, as long as for extending the deadline the exchange is not increased more than if it were arranged for the nearest fair, because it is considered a service and an act of charity to grant a greater time to pay without an increment, something the pope has no intention of prohibiting.

A God-fearing merchant from Lisbon who did not concede exchanges but for the next fair, according to what Pius V's bull ordered, asked me about this. "You should know," he said, "that the instrument we merchants negotiate and obtain profit with is money. And the longer you have to wait at one place until the next fair, the greater the number of merchants who take exchanges for that date, and the less time there is until the fair, the fewer the merchants who want exchanges for that place, and with lower increments. That is why, if the fair of Medina (for example) is celebrated in four months, the exchange market for that fair would be regularly more expensive than after one month went by and, after only one month went by more expensive than two months gone by, so that, ordinarily, the less time there is until the fair, the lower the increment that is given or taken for the exchanges. The reason for this is that the longer the payment for the exchange is deferred, the greater the increment that is given and taken because of the greater profit for the merchants; and the less it is deferred, so much less is given, because of the lower profit for the merchants."

"My question," asked the merchant, "is the following: When there is a longer period of time until the next fair, may I licitly receive all the increment that is currently offered in the exchange market, or should I refrain from such great increment for considering I have received it for the greater delay in payment, and for this reason, in a usurious way? If I have to refrain," he added, "no one will want to grant the exchange in those conditions, as we merchants negotiate and make a profit with money. And if the God-fearing among us refuse to grant those exchanges, only the greedy shall take advantage of them, and consequently since those who grant the exchanges shall be fewer and many more those who solicit it, such increment shall increase, a thing not only detrimental to the God-fearing but also harmful to the public affairs and to those who solicit exchanges."

I answered that there is no reason why one should refrain from carrying out those exchanges at the current market price, as the abundance of solicitors shall make the price increase, if not for reason of the transfer of money, then for other rulings that we will shortly discuss. And the fact that this is the current price in the public market greatly contributes to considering it just. We should add that the scarceness of merchants who give and take money to exchange, and the profit obtained when dealing with money are circumstances that make the price of exchange rise, even for those who take the exchange not for negotiating and earning money but with other ends in mind.

The doctors agree that everything received in excess of the capital when money was given to someone else to be given back with an increment in another place where, however, he does not have money nor anyone to pay for him, but it is presumed that it shall be paid with the increment in the same place where the exchange was carried out, is usurious and subject to restitution. This is the kind of exchange the nobles receive in the Spanish territories to pay, for example, in Flanders or in France with the usual increment for the exchanges for those places, where they neither have money nor anyone to pay for them.

In view of the fact that in this type of exchange money is not transferred—whether formally or virtually—and no one who has money in a place is released of the effort of taking it to the place where he took the exchange—as there is not even an exchange of money in one place for money in another, but of money here for money also here—it is evident that to receive an increment should be considered usurious or dry exchange, as something would be charged for reason of delay or deferment of payment.

There is even greater injustice in allowing such individuals, in the case of not being able to pay in the place and time established beforehand, to reexchange the bills of exchange from that place to this one with a new increment. In such a contract there are two unjust exchanges with obligation to restitute both increments. And the banker may not excuse himself by writing to the place for which he gave the first exchange saying it is the people who took the exchange and did not pay it there who are to blame for the absence of payment, because he was willing to receive the money there. So say, among others, Cajetan and Silvestre.[5] Today Pius V thus defines it at the beginning of the bull on exchanges.

In Portugal, King Sebastian established in law in 1570 that whoever carries out an exchange in such way is subject to the penalty of losing *ipso facto* the totality of what he hands over. And the person who takes the exchange may not waive the right this law grants him, and even if he were to pay, he or his heirs could claim what was thus handed over. It also established severe penalties for the person who received an exchange under these conditions and gave back something to the banker in money or an equivalent. And the law he later promulgated regarding these exchanges, in 1577, does not modify this opinion in anything.

Navarrus and Silvestre[6] say that in order for the exchange not to be usurious and dry, it is sufficient that, even if the person who receives it for a certain place does not have at the moment of receiving the exchange neither money nor someone to answer for him there, it is probable that he shall have it by the time that has been set for payment, which will allow him to pay it, whether because he hopes to obtain the money through a loan or because he shall take it with interest for another place, or in any other way. I believe, however, that this should be understood when

5. Cajetan, *De cambiis*, cap. 1; Soto, *De iustitia et iure*, lib. 6, q. 10, art. 1; Azpilcueta, *Manual*, cap. 17, no. 290; *Comentario*, cap. últ., no. 25; Silvestre, *Summa*, verba usura, 4, q. 9, pronum. 5.

6. Azpilcueta, *Comentario*, cap. últ., no. 14; Silvestre, *Summa*, q. cit., pronum. 7.

he is hoping to obtain the money from a third party and not from the person whom he has to pay or from his representative.

What happens if the banker gave money in exchange for a certain place to someone he thought could pay him there, but then it happens that said person has no money or representative there but will pay in the same place where he received the exchange? May the banker justly accept in this case the increment on the exchange in the same place where he delivered the money? Whatever others may say, I believe the banker may receive in this case, not only compensation for damages and losses he has suffered for giving him the money—because if he had not given it to him he could have given it to someone else in exchange or he could have used the money in some other respectable business—but also, even if they are small losses he may receive an amount as compensation for the opportunity he has missed for using the money that he should have received together with the increment in the preestablished place. And he may obligate the person who took the exchange to put that money with the increment at his own expense in the preestablished place, if that were possible. I believe this because the contract was licit in itself, entered into in good faith on the part of the banker, who furthermore has fulfilled it. And because it is not an innominate contract, it may force the other contracting party to fulfill his part, if he is able to fulfill it, or if he is not able to, to pay in the place where they are the total amount of what the banker would have paid for the contract to be fulfilled in that other place, according to the legal dispositions. This was said in argument 253 and, especially, in 255. And this is valid not only in conscience but also in a court of law.

Although if there are any signs that the banker knew or should have known that the person with whom he was dealing did not have any money or representative in that other place, the contract shall be condemned as usurious in a court of law, and the banker shall be liable to the usurers' penalties. What has been said may be confirmed, because frauds and tricks should not benefit their instigators. And also, as said in arguments 327 and 380, the sale of something belonging to someone else on the thief's part is a valid contract, not in the sense that the buyer acquires the property of the thing, but in the sense that the thief, in case of eviction, is responsible as long as it is convenient to the buyer that the thief be considered owner of the thing. What we said in argument 352, regarding someone who in good faith brought some oxen to a supposed owner who was renting them, is in accordance with the above.

Argument 405

Answers to Some Questions Regarding What Has Been Said in the Two Preceding Arguments

What Can Be Said About Those Who for a Salary Bring with Them the Horses They Needed to Rent for the Trip

Is It Licit to Receive an Increment for the Exchange Carried Out from One Place to Another within the Same Kingdom?

First question: There is uncertainty as to whether the two types of exchange we have explained in the two preceding arguments, in which an increment over the principal was collected, are licit not only for public bankers whose job it is to practice exchanges, but also for the regular citizens. The answer is affirmative, because the service rendered in favor of the one who asks for the exchange is worth that increment, whoever the person is who renders the service, and there is no law prohibiting the exercise of such a type of exchange to regular citizens.

Second question: Let us suppose that someone had money, let us say, in Lisbon, and had to transfer it to Flanders to buy some goods, pay some debts, or with some other end in mind. And let us suppose this person had thought of giving it to a merchant so he returned it in Flanders with some kind of discount. Finally, let us suppose some other person came along who needed in Lisbon the money he had in Flanders and asked the first person to exchange the money he had in Lisbon for the one the other had in Flanders, for which he would pay an increment. May the person who has his money in Lisbon licitly accept the increment they are offering him, given that he is very interested in transferring the money from Lisbon to Flanders, just as the other is in bringing his from Flanders to Lisbon? The answer has to be affirmative, as the service he carries out for the other person is really worth that increment, and if that happens to be to his advantage, it is something that occurs *per accidens*. In contracts, what matters to determine if they are just or not is if what one person does is equivalent to what he receives from the other in compensation, and this is what happens in our situation, as affirm Soto and Medina.[1]

Something similar happens when someone takes to a particular place a horse that he rented and that he had to give back to the owner, incurring certain expenses. If he found a third person who was willing to rent the horse to travel to the place of origin, he may licitly rent it for a just price, without there being an impediment that in so doing he saves money for the expenses he would incur in order to return the horse. And since there is equality between the use of the horse, which is what is granted, and the price that is paid for it, the contract thus entered shall be just, even if on the other hand, and *per accidens*, he obtains an economic advantage.

Similarly, I believe the following: Let us suppose that someone decided to rent a horse to travel to a certain place and found someone else who, without knowing of this trip, wished to hire him to take a horse to that same place. It must be said that he may licitly rent out his services and receive a just stipend for the job of taking the horse, without it being an impediment for doing so that he is taking the horse to the same place he was thinking of traveling, saving money on what he would have spent to rent the horse himself. The reason is the same as above: that the service he renders the other person deserves remuneration, even if *per*

1. Domingo de Soto, *De iustitia et iure, libri decem* (Salamanca, 1553), lib. 6, q. 10, art. 1; Juan de Medina, *De cambiis* (Salamanca, 1550), q. 5.

accidens it brings to him a greater advantage. I also say that if one were looking for someone to take a horse to a certain place and found out that another person has a need of a horse in that same place, both could agree to mutually render themselves the service, reciprocally absolving themselves from the total or partial price, as what is agreed between them shall be considered just. The reason is that neither one is obliged to enter into the agreement in order to benefit the other, nor needs to mix the contract in which they agree to render a service with another different contract. But if for reason of the personal need that is simultaneously satisfied one of them wanted to give a discount or reduction, it is something he may do. The same must be said about two merchants who know of the mutual need of transferring money from one place to another.

What was said above is consistent with strict justice and theoretical strictness, though moral and fraternal charity reasons may suggest loosening up that strictness. However, one may not condemn as guilty the person who does not wish to loosen up his position; or at least, he may not be accused of mortal sin.

In the cited issue, Juan de Medina affirms that if someone needing 1,000 *ducats* in Flanders gives them to a merchant in the Spanish territories so that he looks for someone who wants to receive them in exchange and give them back in Flanders with an increment, he would commit usury, because in doing so he would put his money in Flanders with a profit for himself. I do not see how this may be judged as usurious since, in truth, the owner of the money uses the right he has to give it for an exchange, this being an operation in which anyone else who did not need money in Flanders could make a profit on it. And the fact that *per accidens* his money is transferred to Flanders as he expected, does not make that contract illicit, as we have already explained and Medina himself concedes. The fact that there is an invitation to directly or indirectly practice a money exchange—which in all other respects is just—does not make it illicit either.

As for the last part of the argument, namely, whether it is licit to receive an increase or benefit for the exchange carried out from one place to another in the same kingdom, as would be from Seville to Medina, even if Soto denies it, doctor Navarrus affirms it in the earlier cited *Comentario*,[2] and argues that it is by nature licit as long as the increment is moderate and proportional to the distance. I fully agree with his opinion, and it may be proved correct in the following way: If the activity of carrying money from one place to another outside the kingdom deserves remuneration, the same goes for carrying it within the kingdom itself, although it should be less significant if the distance is shorter and the dangers of transportation fewer, especially since there is no prohibition to transport the money within the kingdom itself as there usually is to take it out of it. And so we see that the students' errand boys justly charge their price for the formal transportation of money, and they may charge it even if they do not transport the money materially but only in a virtual way, receiving it in one place and later handing it over at the students' residence place. I do not believe Soto had any intention of denying this, but only that that transportation did not deserve such high prices as the merchants usually charged the nobles for picking up the money they gave them in the king's court to take it to the place where the nobles have their income and residence. This is the way merchants usually conceal usuries.

Even if this is so by nature, both the citizens as well as the foreigners in this kingdom are forbidden from giving money in exchange in order to take it from one place to another in the kingdom with an increment or interest, or to take it to a fair carried out in the same kingdom.[3] The penalty established is the loss of all the money for the person who received it in ex-

2. Soto, *De iustitia et iure*, lib. 6, q. 10, art. 1; Martín de Azpilcueta, *Manual de confesores y penitentes* (Salamanca, 1556), cap. 17, no. 290; Azpilcueta, *Comentario resolutorio de usuras* (Salamanca, 1556), cap. final, no. 28.

3. N. R. 5.18.8 (Ed. note: Cf. N. N. R. 9.3.3).

change, and all the penalties established against the usurers for the person who gave it.

In Portugal, instead, even if King Sebastian prohibited these same actions in the law he promulgated in 1570, he later allowed them in those cases in which the money was received in one of the four fairs he established in Portugal (and which were never carried out) in order to reimburse it in one of those other fairs, or when the money was received some place other than where the fairs took place in order to pay it in the following fair. Apart from this, the same king Sebastian, in one of his resolutions prior to the 1577 law (of which I have a copy), revoked that first law from 1570 in regards to the exchanges considered licit according to Pius V's bull, the Portuguese law, and the natural law. The result of which is that in Portugal today it is not illicit to exchange from one place to another in the kingdom, charging an increment, as long as this is moderate.

In the places cited earlier, Navarrus says these laws that prohibit the exchange of money between places in the same kingdom should apply only to the cases in which the banker hands over the money first and later receives it with an increment somewhere else, as there may be concealed usury, such as for example, if the increment were received for reason of the loan being made, or the delay in payment, but that the laws should not apply when the banker first receives the money that he shall give back later somewhere else as, in this case, there is no danger of committing usury or of concealing it. However, the prohibition in these cases could be an impediment for transferring the money from one place to another, thus being detrimental to the regular citizens and to the common good. I believe the law of Castile cited earlier does not apply to these cases due to the fact that in them money is not given for an interest, the activity that such a law expects to correct.

It is worth asking oneself if in the case that someone—against what these laws regulate—received for the exchange carried out from one place to another a retribution that would be considered licit and just if it were not for such laws, he would be forced to restitute such amount *ipso facto*, that is, even before the judicial decision was issued. My opinion is that the answer is no, because, in truth, the service rendered is worth what has been received for it. Even if the contract were null for reason of such laws (which does not seem to be the sense of the cited law of Castile, which only prohibits doing it under severe penalties), the person receiving the money would not be forced to give it back before a judicial sentence was issued forcing him to, and not without taking before a just compensation for the service rendered gratuitously. What happens in this case is the same as in those contracts where some goods are exchanged for others: If the contract is annulled, the one who carried it out does not have to give back what he received if he in turn does not get back what he gave, or is compensated for it. And even if the law enforced it, in this matter it should be considered as mere penal law, which would lack power in the conscience's realm before the judicial sentence was issued.

ARGUMENT 406

ON HOW THE SAME AMOUNT OF MONEY MAY HAVE A DIFFERENT VALUE IN DIFFERENT PLACES

In the three preceding arguments we have examined one of the rulings or reasons for which it may be licit to charge an increment over the principal for the exchange carried out from one place to another. Before examining two other reasons for which this type of exchange may be licitly practiced we must explain the issue before us.

The same amount of money may have more value in one place than in another in two ways: first, because according to the law or accepted custom it has, in comparison to other coins, a different value in places that are also different. Thus, for example, a *ducat* is worth 400 *reais* in Portugal and 375 *maravedis* in Castile; and a silver *real* is worth 34 *maravedis* in Castile and today it is worth 40 in Portugal. And in the kingdom of Valencia the *real* is worth fewer *dines* than in Cataluña. The *dines* are the smallest common copper coins in those kingdoms. In other places, the *real* has different values. Consequently, 11 silver *reales* are worth 374 *maravedis* in Castile, and in Portugal they are worth today 440 *reais*, disregarding other places for the time being. The gold *escudo*, which in the past was worth in Castile 10 silver *reales* and 10 *maravedis*, that is, 350 *maravedis*, was worth in Rome 11½ *julios* (the *julio* is equivalent to the silver *real*), and in France and in other places it had different values. Today, in Castile, its value has increased to 400 *maravedis*.

There is another way money may have more value in one place than in another, namely, when it is more abundant. In equal circumstances, the more abundant money is in one place, so much less is its value to buy things or to acquire things that are not money. Just as the abundance of merchandise reduces their price when the amount of money and quantity of merchants remains invariable, so too the abundance of money makes prices rise when the amount of merchandise and number of merchants remain invariable, to the point where the same money loses purchasing power. So we see that, in the present day, money is worth in the Spanish territories much less than what it was worth eighty years ago, due to the abundance of it. What was bought before for two today is bought for five, or for six, or maybe for more. The price of salaries has risen in the same proportion, as well as dowries and the value of real estate, revenues, benefices, and all other things. That is exactly why we see that money is worth much less in the New World, especially in Peru, than in the Spanish territories, due to its abundance. And wherever money is less abundant than in the Spanish territories, it is worth more. Neither is it worth the same in all parts because of this reason, yet it varies according to its abundance and all other circumstances. This value does not remain unaltered as if it were indivisible but fluctuates within the limits defined by the people's estimation, the same as happens with merchandise not appraised by law. This money's value is not the same in all parts of the Spanish territories, but different, as ordinarily it is worth less in Seville—where the ships arrive from the New World and where for that reason there is usually an abundance of it—than in other places of the same Spanish territories.

In addition to this, the greater the need for money there is in one place—for example, to buy merchandise, war expenses, the royal court's expenditures, or for any other reason—the more it is worth there than in other places. What is more, these same reasons make money worth more at some times than in others in one and the same place. Money that in one place is exchanged for money in another place functions as merchandise not appraised by law, whose value rises at some times and falls at others, depending on whether there is more or less need of it. That is why the abundance of one type of merchandise, the greater or lesser need of it and the greater or lesser number of merchants who want it, make its value rise or fall in a particular place. This is exactly what happens with money: its greater or lesser abundance in one place, the need there is of it, the greater or lesser number of those who want to exchange it for diverse places and of those who can and want to accept those exchanges, are the reasons for which money at a certain time is worth more in one place than in another, or at different times. And even in the same fair and in one and the same place, it shall be worth more or less according to whether at the beginning, middle, or end of the fair there are more or fewer people who need money and want to take it in exchange for other places, and more or fewer people who want to hand it over.

When in the kingdoms and republics the value of larger coins is appraised in relation to the smaller ones, such a rate applies only to the exchange of some coins for others in the same place and in the purchase of goods in that place. The kingdoms and republics have never wanted to appraise the coins as far as the value we are referring to now, that is, to exchange them for coins in other places, as this value is not constant, even if the other type of value is appraised by law. And because it is a just value even after the legal appraisal, appraising the coins in order to exchange them for coins from other places would be to the disadvantage of kingdoms and republics, whose merchandise would start going scarce due to this appraisal. That is why the custom has always rightfully, and notwithstanding the appraised price, respected the fact that coins had this other variable value when exchanging them for coins in other places. And in his bull, Pius V approved this type of exchange with an increment.

I explained that the money from one place that is exchanged for money in another functions as a merchandise not appraised by law, because concerning the place where it is, it always retains the value appraised by law or accepted by custom. For even if in Medina or in any other place where exchanges are usually taken, the value of money varies because the exchange is given more expensively for one place than for another, and even in one and the same place the exchange is given more expensively to some people than to others due to the fact that it is not indivisible and during the same fair it may vary according to the circumstances. However, in comparison to Medina itself and to the merchandise bought there at different times or to pay debts, it always maintains the price appraised by law—and according to that price merchandise is bought and debts are paid—even if that other value of the coin increases or diminishes. What is more, in all the places where the exchange has to be compensated, the amount of money to be paid according to the contract is always estimated according to the value appraised by the law for the money in that place.

Argument 407

If Coins That by Law or Generally Accepted Custom Had a Different Value in Relation to Other Copper Coins of a Lesser Value in Places Also Different, Can They Be Justly Exchanged between Those Places Keeping to the Equality?

The issue is of great utility and it is worth knowing, considering that the practice of the merchants and the doctrine of many doctors do not agree with each other. Some look for weak ploys and try to make them prevail in order not to condemn the practice in some places, this being so that if their main assertion were true, such practice would be usurious, especially if the banker gives the money first so that it is later returned to him in another place. Consider that in this argument we are not discussing the increment the banker may licitly charge for reason of the exchange, nor the rulings that allow him to licitly charge it. We are discussing the commutation itself (putting aside such rulings and such increment) and want to know whether there is an equality when money that is worth less in comparison to the small copper coins is exchanged for the same money to be delivered in a place where it is worth more in comparison to the copper coins, or whether, conversely, there is no equality in such practice, and such excess or difference must be compensated for there to be equality in the contract, and thus, whether the one changing the money in the place where it is worth less should reduce the exchange of the similar coins that he has to give back in another place—and vice versa, whether the one who carries out the exchange where they are worth more can and should increase the respective increment in the exchange.

Some examples: When the *ducat* began to be minted, it was worth in Castile 375 *maravedis*, in Portugal 400 *reais* and, in Flanders, its value in what they call *gruesos* in that province was equivalent to 400 *reais* or *maravedis*, according to the estimation of the merchants and to the consensus in exchanges and in all negotiations. But since today there is no coin with precisely that value—as said in argument 400—the *ducat*'s value in these three regions is still the same to the present day, whatever the coin used to pay. What is more, if in the exchanges or in any other business or contract, the *ducat* is suddenly mentioned for any reason, its value is understood to be in Castile 375 *maravedis*, and in Portugal and in Flanders 400 *reais* or *maravedis*. The question, therefore, is: When those gold coins had that value in former times, and when today, since they no longer exist, they speak of *ducats* in the exchanges making reference to the explained value, do they observe the equality when exchanging a *ducat* in Castile for a *ducat* in Portugal or in Flanders? And vice versa, when a *ducat* in Portugal or in Flanders is exchanged for a *ducat* in Castile, do they observe that equality?

Another example is that of the silver *reales* that in Castile are worth 34 *maravedis*, in Portugal 40, and in the kingdom of Valencia are worth a lower amount of *dines* than in Cataluña (the so called *dines* are each worth 1½ *maravedi*). The question is: Is due equality observed if 100 *reales* in Castile are commuted or exchanged for the same number in Portugal, or the other way around—100 in Portugal for the same amount in Castile? Or, in a similar way, 100 *reales* in Valencia for the same amount in Barcelona, and the other way around? The result is a much greater increment for the *ducat*, as 375 *maravedis* make in Castile 11 silver *reales* with 1 *maravedi*, and in Portugal 400 *reais* make only 10 silver *reales*. The question is: Is due equality observed in the commutation or exchange of 100 *ducats* in Castile for the same amount in Portugal, and the other way around—100 in Portugal for the same amount in Castile? For if the value of a coin in comparison to the small copper coins is in one place greater than in another, but they are considered equal in the exchange from one place to another, we have here a new ruling for which an increment may be taken through the exchange from the place where it is worth more to the place where it is worth less, and for reason of which the exchange shall have to be reduced, in order to make it on both parts equitable and just when carried out from the place where it is worth less to the place where it is worth more.

Navarrus believes that if someone gives 100 *ducats* in Castile to get the same amount back in Portugal, or if he gives 100 silver *reales* in Castile to get back the same amount in Portugal, it is not a commutation on equal terms but an unjust and usurious loan,[1] because, he says, the *ducat* and the silver *real* are worth more in Portugal than in Castile; and he refers to the time when the silver *real* was worth a little more than 36 *reais* in Portugal, and when the *ducat* was worth 11 silver *reales*, which amount to 400 *reais*. And Navarrus would say the same in the other examples we have included. Others who wrote after him were of the same opinion.

Even if Soto is of the same opinion when the same coin is worth more in one place than in another,[2] and gives the example of a *ducat* worth more silver *reales* in Italy than in the Spanish territories, when the *reales* have all the same value, or the *ducat* is worth more *gruesos* in one place than in another, I do not know, however, whether he would say the same in the examples we have included.

---

1. Martín de Azpilcueta, *Manual de confesores y penitentes* (Salamanca, 1556), cap. 17, no. 295; Azpilcueta, *Comentario resolutorio de usuras* (Salamanca, 1556), cap. últ, nos. 60 and 61.

2. Domingo de Soto, *De iustitia et iure, libri decem* (Salamanca, 1553), lib. 6, q. 12, art. 1.

Navarrus' argumentation: The copper coin called *real* in Portugal has the same value as the Castilian *maravedi*. For in the same way that said copper coin is worth in Portugal 6 *ceptis*, and half of it is worth 3, in Castile too, in the time where they had *cornados* and *meajas*, 6 of these were worth 1 *maravedi*, and 3 were worth half, which in Castile they call *blanca*. Today, in the kingdom of Galicia, 6 *cornados* are worth 1 *maravedi*. Therefore, since the value of the *maravedi* and that of the Portuguese copper *real* are the same, it is unjust to receive in Portugal 1 silver real with a value of 36 *maravedis* for 1 silver *real* received in Castile with a value of 34 *maravedis*. And it shall also be unjust to receive in Portugal 1 *ducat* of 400 *reais* for a *ducat* worth 374 *maravedis* received in Castile.

This may be proved as follows: If one and the same measure of wheat is worth more in Portugal than in Castile, as usually happens, it is certainly unjust to commute one measure of wheat in Castile for an equal one in Portugal, even if the wheat from Castile is better than that of Portugal. And it would be usury to be loaned one measure of wheat in Castile for an equal one in Portugal, since the value of the one received in Portugal is greater than the loan of wheat given in Castile. For this same reason there shall be injustice and usury, with obligation to restitute, if a loan of 100 silver *reales* or 100 *ducats* is received in Castile for a same amount to be given back in Portugal, since more would be given back in Portugal than what was received in Castile.

Contrary to this, and which always has been, is the practice of merchants who are more familiar with the estimation of goods than the scholastic doctors, and whose judgment we should abide by in these matters, especially when applied to the dealings they carry out with one another in which none of them complain or object. In the issue set forth concerning commuting money from one place to another, the merchants refer to the silver or gold coins which, taken from one place, maintain their value in all parts, more than to the copper ones, because these—as coins—ordinarily have a different value in the various kingdoms and regions. And the coin that is valuable in one place has no value in another, and for reason of the copper they possess they are worth almost nothing, because of which the expense of taking them from one place to another exceeds the value of the copper they are made of. That is why the merchants, for their exchanges and dealings from one place to another, do not take the small copper coins as standard to measure the value of those made of gold and silver, but on the contrary, they make gold and silver the measure of value of the copper coins in that place. That is why, in many places, they carry out the exchanges for diverse places using as unity the silver *marcas* (which we call *marcos* and the Latin *selibras*). And when they carry out the exchanges in *ducats* or *escudos*, as they were usually carried out for the Spanish territories or from the Spanish territories, given that the silver *real* was readily accepted in all places and the majority of the exchanges were paid off with it, they decided that when dealing from one place to another, the silver *real* would have the same value in all places. That is why, since that *real* has a different value in different places due to appraisal or custom, they decided that the small copper coins that in different places have been made the measure of the silver *real* (and, consequently, of the *ducat* and the *escudo*) should not have the same value to buy merchandise in that region, nor to pay debts or carry out exchanges of small coins for other bigger ones. The value of small copper coins is different in the proportion in which the number of copper coins given for a silver *real* in one region exceeds the amount of coins given for it in another region. And so, among merchants, it was decided that the *maravedi* from Castile should be worth more than the Portuguese *real*. And today, in comparison to the same Portuguese coin, it has a much greater value than before, because the Portuguese silver *real* has increased its value to 40 *reais* from the 36 *reais* it was worth before.

The merchants are of the same opinion regarding the *maravedis* in Castile in comparison to the *gruesos* in Flanders, and the same should be said about the copper *denarios* from the kingdom of Valencia in comparison to the copper *denarios* from Cataluña. In agreement with this opinion is the law Charles V promulgated on exchanges, according to what Navarrus[3] says when he states that 375 *maravedis* from Castile are worth in Portugal 400 *reais*, when he is talking about the time before the silver *real* was worth in Portugal 40 *reais*. And even if Navarrus, in the cited number 60, says one should not abide by such law, the truth is quite the contrary, as it is reasonable and such law is supported by the general opinion and the merchants' practice, which has so much weight to determine the just price of things. Another substantial argument is the one saying that the more copper coins that, according to the law, should be given for a silver *real* and for other silver and gold coins, the lower the price of the small copper coins. Experience showed in Portugal that as soon as the silver *real* increased to 40 *reais*, there was an immediate increase of the price of things expressed in those small copper coins.

If Navarrus' opinion were true, today usury would be carried out by the person who gave a loan of 1,100 silver *reales* in Castile in order to get back only 1,000 in Portugal, or what is the same, the person who gave a loan of 100 *ducats* and 11 silver *reales* in exchange for only 110 *reales* to be received in Portugal. This would be usury, and the person who gave the money in Castile would be forced to restitute 26 *maravedis* for each *ducat*, because 11 *reales* of each *ducat* he loans are worth in Castile 374 *maravedis*, whereas for the 10 *reales* he receives in Portugal he would receive 400 *reais*. And if these have the same value as the Castilian *maravedi*, our man would receive in Portugal 26 extra *maravedis* for each *ducat* given in Castile. Who is the fool who would be willing to give in Castile 11 silver *reales* and 26 *maravedis* in exchange for only 10 silver *reales* he would receive in Portugal? Or who would accept in Portugal only 10 *reales* in exchange for 11 and 26 *maravedis* he would have to give back in

3. Azpilcueta, *Comentario*, cap. últ., no. 30.

Castile? Is there anyone who can be persuaded that such contract is equitable and just? I do not think so.

But one should take into account that such increase in the value of the gold and silver coins in relation to those of copper in the province itself where the increment is decided upon has a certain importance, since from then on those coins shall be used to pay greater debts than before, and it shall be possible to buy more goods than before. As that is the reason why more silver and gold coins of that type arrive from other regions: something is gained from bringing them to this province. Because of this, such increase slightly reduces the price of bartering and exchanging said coins from the place where they are worth more.

Regarding this there cannot be a better rule than to pay attention to the current price in the exchange market, and to the exchanges the merchants carry out among themselves from one place to another, and to accept that price as just and accepted by the merchants' common estimation. It should be noted that after the value of the silver *real* increased to 400 *reais*, and 10 *reales* amount to 1 *ducat* of 400 *reais*, if changes are made from Portugal to Castile or from Castile to Portugal taking the *ducat* as unity (as was usually done before), one should note that the exchange from Portugal to Castile has lost almost the eleventh part of its old value in the same way that the *ducat* has diminished in an eleventh fraction. On the contrary, the exchange from Castile to Portugal increased by almost an eleventh part of the amount that the Castilian *ducat* exceeds the Portuguese *ducat*.

There are, however, today some Portuguese who grant exchanges from Lisbon to Medina for an equal amount of *ducats* and wait to be paid a whole year, which is manifest usury and explains why when I was in Lisbon a certain God-fearing merchant from Medina warned us to be against this type of usury and ruin to one's own conscience. For if such is the way 100 *ducats* are given in exchange in Lisbon, it turns out that for 1,000 silver *reales* that are given in Lisbon they want to be paid 1,100 in Medina after a year's time, deceiving other learned men by saying they have granted exchanges on an equal basis, that is, a *ducat* for a *ducat*, but without telling them that the Castilian *ducat* exceeds the Portuguese *ducat* in the eleventh part of its value. And the confessors pay no heed to this.

To Navarrus' argument we answer by denying that the Portuguese copper *real* has the same value as the Castilian *maravedi* when the exchanges are from one place to another. For even if in the past 1 was worth 6 copper coins, called *ceptis* in Portugal, and *cornados* and *meajas* in Castile, when the silver *real* increased its value in Portugal in comparison to those copper coins, the value of these—called *reais* and *ceptis*—diminished in the same proportion in comparison to the *maravedis* that in the past were called *cornados* and *meajas* in Castile, as has already been explained. We admit the antecedent and deny the consequent for the argument of confirmation, as we have already explained that the *ducat* was never more valuable in Portugal than in Castile, and today it is worth much less.

ARGUMENT 408

ON THE PEOPLE WHO TRAVEL FROM ONE PLACE TO ANOTHER TO CARRY OUT EXCHANGES

Before embarking upon the last reason for which in the exchange of money from one place to another the price may licitly be increased and sometimes it is better to reduce it, we must explain a few practical issues on exchanges, which shall put an end to this subject, and before anything else, we must explain who is involved in the business of exchanging.

Three types of people, who depend on each other, are involved in the exchanges. One type are the merchants, who on their own or through their own delegated employees (whom they call *factores*), or through correspondents, practice trading in different places—such as Lisbon, Seville, Medina, Flanders, Genoa, Florence, Venetia, the Green Promontory, the Isle of Santo Tomé, several places in the New World, the East Indies, and other similar places—taking from one place the things that are worth more in others and sending to the first ones those that are more valuable there. The following examples shall make it clearer. From Portugal they send to Flanders oil, salt, wine, pepper, and other things that arrive in Portugal from the East Indies, Brazil, and other lands in the Portuguese trading area.

From Flanders they bring to Portugal all the things necessary in Portugal itself, and in the East Indies, Brazil, and all the other regions that trade with Portugal. There is a similar commerce between the kingdom of Portugal and the several provinces and cities of the Spanish territories, France, Italy, and so forth. From there they bring paper, books, silk, scarlet fabrics they call *rajas*, and the rest of the merchandise that is necessary in the kingdom of Portugal and in the provinces of its commercial area. And, in turn, from Portugal they send to those places those things that from Portugal and its commercial area are offered with an advantage. To Seville they bring from many provinces and cities in Europe those things that are typical of these places, and from diverse places in the New World and the Islands of the Ocean, subject to the crown of Castile. From Seville, in turn, they send to several provinces the things that there is abundance of in Seville, namely, in addition to money and great quantities of gold and silver that arrive there from the commerce with the New World, other innumerable merchandise, characteristic of the Betica[1] or, particularly, brought from various places across the sea. Other similar examples may be found in other provinces and cities. Consequently, the most important merchants of each province do business in several places, so that at times they are owed money for the merchandise they have sent and at others it is they who owe money for the merchandise they have bought and carried away. At times they are in need of money, and at others they have an abundance thereof. That is why, in all those places they need employees, correspondents, and what they call credit, that is, people who accept their bills of exchange in that place and pay the amounts they order and who receive the amounts that other similar bills of exchange order to be given to them, managing their business in that place.

From all this multiple and varied negotiation they carry out in diverse places it often comes to pass that merchants need for

1. Ed. note: *Bética*: relative to that old Roman province, today Andalucía.

their dealings and profits the money they have in other places in abundance, which gave origin to the practice that whoever needed money in one place demanded of those who had it there in abundance to exchange it for the money they had somewhere else, or for a place where they could pay more easily. Thus, the merchants helped each other in the exchanges to facilitate their dealings and profits. This was the beginning of the exchanges between merchants, the only ones who practiced them among themselves. However, the exchange usually resulted in a profit in the place where it was remunerated, whether because the exchange itself deserved that the person carrying it out would benefit from it, as was proved before, or because ordinarily those to whom the money was given in exchange by doing business and buying merchandise to take to other places where it was worth more obtained a much greater profit than those who had given them the money. Consequently, anyone who had money, attracted by the chance of profit they saw in the exchange and by the safety of the business and the little effort, started to help merchants in the main business centers and to give them money in exchange, in different places in their own name or in the name of their employees and correspondents. And this business was so profitable that, exercised with ability, it brought about a great amount of money to the places where, for its very conditions, they expected it would be worth more. They even took money in exchange with a small interest for those places from which they could later give it in exchange for other places with a greater interest. And so it happened that many people ceased trading to dedicate themselves entirely to the business of exchange. And this is the second type of people involved in the practice of exchanges. They happen to be only—or mainly—exchange dealers by profession, who help the merchants in one way or another and depend on them in their business.

These people need to have their correspondents in the places where they practice trading and grant the exchanges, no less than the merchants. They also need to have credit there, for which they need people in those places to whom they can send bills of exchange to be cashed in that place, and who in their name the exchange dealers give the money they have there for exchanges, whether for the place where the main banker lives or for another where the increment is greater or is expected to be in the future. All according to the orders received or to whatever they deem more convenient according to the circumstances.

Also the main exchange dealers often need to exchange money in the place where they are in order to take it to other places where they can make a greater profit with it in new exchanges drawn to other places, or to transfer it through successive exchanges to the place where they shall need it and expect it shall be worth more, or for other reasons of usefulness or convenience. Frequently, it is also true that they find it useful and necessary to take money in exchange in other places, whether because they need the money to pay for the exchanges they bought for that place or to send it through successive exchanges to the places where they shall need it because they think it shall be worth more there. For these and other reasons, the main exchange dealer, no less than the merchants themselves, need correspondents and credit in several places.

This negotiating with exchanges is frequently carried out with credit, obtaining great profit, more so than using one's own money in cash, even though having a lot of money in different places greatly contributes to success. For even if an exchange dealer does not have much money, if he has credit and correspondents in several places and is also skillful, he can give orders so that in his name his correspondents take money in exchange at those times when it is worth less in order to take it to those other places where it is worth more and where he will be able to pay for them more easily. And then he can order again to give a certain amount of money in exchange with a greater increment at a time when it is worth more or for those places where it shall be worth more or is expected to be worth more. And so, taking in exchange money from some and giving it to others, they can make a great profit with the money that initially was taken in exchange.

In a similar way, an exchange dealer has a special ability to speculate on the time and place in which money shall be worth much more for its scarcity and for the need merchants and many others shall have of it: For example, when the prince in that place is preparing for a war and collects all the money of the region, whence it is likely believed that the merchants of the fairs in that region will have great need of that money as not rarely happened in Flanders when Charles V dwelt there. If our exchange dealer in addition to foresight had the ability to transport through successive exchanges a great amount of money to have it ready at the correct time and place, he shall be able to obtain great profits by giving money in exchange with large increments for the places from where he took it, and on the fourth month, or later, he shall recover the money in a much greater quantity in the same places.

The third type of men who dedicate themselves to the business of exchanges are those called bankers. Their job, in those places where commerce and exchanging are the main activities, consists of receiving the money that the merchants and exchange dealers deposit in their bank and, being trustees of that money, paying the amount of money ordered by the depositors, keeping a written account of all the amounts received and given under their orders, and having the tally with their dealings with other clients always ready. Before they assume their responsibilities, these men have to bring in guarantors and post a legal bond in those republics where they are to practice their occupation as guarantee that they will practice their occupation with integrity and pay the whole amount of what they receive in deposit.

These bankers, says Mercado, are somewhat different in Seville and in the places where they celebrate fairs, such as Medina and other similar places, because in Seville, there are so many advantages to such deposits that they do not receive any other retribution, and they still consider it no small benefit that merchants and exchange dealers want to deposit their money in the bank and utilize their services in that region. Navarrus says this is also what happens in Rome and in some places of the Gaul and the Spanish territories,[2] because the bankers, with the money that has been deposited, sometimes make a profit of 2,000 or 3,000 *ducats* in three or four months, giving it for exchanges or negotiating with it during the time in which the owners do not need it, or sending merchandise to the New World and other parts, from where they obtain no small profit. Sometimes it happens, though, that when the winds of fortune change they collapse into extreme poverty, being in danger and subject to harm by those they brought in as guarantors. When they are reduced to such poverty that they cannot pay the deposits and other debts, they say the bank has gone bankrupt. But as long as fortune is not so unfavorable to them, since they have deposited the money of many merchants and exchange dealers (from Lisbon, Genoa, Florence, Medina, Toledo, etc.), and from many of these they have many thousands of *ducats,* it never happens that all the depositors need their money so that they do not leave many thousands of *ducats* in deposit, which the bankers can do business with for their benefit or loss, because these bankers, as everybody else, are the true owners of the money that is deposited in their banks, which makes them very different from other depositaries, as we shall explain later when discussing deposits. Consequently, if the money perishes, it perishes for them and not for the depositors, as they receive the money not in custody and to give back the same numerical amount, but to be ready to give back an equal amount whenever the depositor solicits it. Therefore, they receive it as a loan—under temporary use and enjoyment—and, consequently, at their own risk, so that they

2. Martín de Azpilcueta, *Manual de confesores y penitentes* (Salamanca, 1556), cap. 17, no. 293.

return it all at once or in installments when it is required of them and in such way as is required of them.

There are other bankers, especially in the places where fairs are celebrated, who receive the money from those who want to deposit it in their bank. These pay the letters of payment that the depositors send them, give or take money according to their instructions, keep an account of everything given and received and, finally, keep the clients' accounts. For this reason, at the end of the fair they receive from each one of these the price for their work, greater or lesser according to the volume of business carried out. Mercado says that, ordinarily, these commissions furnish each banker with 1,500 or 2,000 *ducats* in each fair.

Regarding the bankers, especially those of the first type, they should be cautioned that they mortally sin if the money they have in trust is engaged in their businesses to such a great degree that they are later unable to give back in due time the amount that the depositors request or send to disburse with a charge from the money they have deposited. Also, they are compelled to restitute the damages, including the profit ceasing, of not having complied with the order they had received to pay. Because the money was received in trust with the obligation of returning it when ordered to do so and, thus, when the time comes and they do not pay, they sin against justice and against the pact they have with the depositors, because of which they shall be compelled to restitute the damages that followed—including the profit ceasing. Also, they mortally sin if they dedicate themselves to the type of transactions where they run the risk of getting involved in a situation where they will be unable to pay for the deposits. For example, if they send such a great amount of merchandise across sea that in case of shipwrecking, or the ship being caught by pirates, it is not possible for them to pay for the deposits, not even by selling their assets. And they not only mortally sin when the business ends badly, but also even if it were to end favorably, and this for reason of the danger they exposed themselves to, causing damage to the depositors and guarantors that they had brought in themselves for the deposits.

Regarding those who deposit their money with those bankers who do not charge anything—either for the deposit or for the rest of services we mentioned before—it is uncertain if the depositors should pay them an adequate stipend (regardless of the fact that the bankers are able to obtain advantages when doing transactions with the money that has been deposited), or, if they do not, commit usury in not paying it. Navarrus responds affirmatively.[3] The following argument apparently proves this opinion: Such deposit is really a loan, as has been said, and the property of the money deposited is transferred to the banker, because of which in case it perishes, it perishes for the banker. Therefore, regardless of the profit the banker manages for himself by dealing skillfully with the money deposited, even if it were a great one, the depositors may not demand nor receive from the banker any money, nor anything that is worth that money, for that deposit and loan. Otherwise, they would commit usury and would have to restitute what they received.

This argument proves that it is about not so much a deposit in favor of the depositor, but a loan in favor of the banker, even if *per accidens* the money that the clients enter into their bank accounts happens to remain in his power, the same as the money of a loan remains in power of the borrower. That is why the argument is not as sound as it would appear on the surface. For, as we said in argument 405, when two people have a simultaneous need, one of returning a horse to a certain place and the other of renting a horse to go to that same place, either one of them may refuse to sign any other contract that is not one that cedes his service in favor of the other, for which he may receive the adequate price even if such contract brings about a great advantage for himself. Likewise, in the issue above, the banker may decide not to receive

3. Martín de Azpilcueta, *Comentario resolutorio de usuras* (Salamanca, 1556), cap. últ., no. 40; Azpilcueta, *Manual*, cap. 17, no. 295.

in his bank the money of others if they do not pay for the rights of custody and pay for the rest of the services he renders, and it shall be no impediment that such deposit shall provide him benefits, namely, that with such money he may carry out transactions and gain a profit. For all of this, the banker may licitly enter an agreement for an adequate stipend for such services and may receive it regardless of obtaining a greater profit.

It should be said, on the contrary, that the merchants and exchange dealers—in view of the profit the banker obtains when dealing with that money and of the need he has of it for making a profit—may not want to enter into any contract with him except a loan in terms that are favorable to the banker and, thus, do him a favor by choosing him over others who would also like to enter the contract. It shall be no impediment to carry this out that with such a loan they manage to protect their money, and they get it back all at once or in installments whenever they want. Therefore, if they only had the intention of entering a loan contract, as they are capable of doing and we presume is their wish, they shall certainly not owe anything to the banker for protecting the money—something linked to the contract *per accidens*—and even if *per accidens* it happens that, as with the rest of the borrowers, they do not owe anything for such protection.

They shall not owe him anything either for the effort or the service of counting the money—either when he receives it or when he pays it—whether it is to the depositors themselves or to others by their orders (just as nothing is owed to other borrowers for these services, as the contract is favorable to them). Neither will they owe the bankers anything for reason of what is given and received, even if it is necessary to write down some documents for this, as the lender does not owe anything to the borrower for the documents that for the debts' security are signed at the time of making or paying the loan for the borrower's own security. For, as the loan is carried out for the benefit of the borrower, it is he who has to pay for all the expenses and not the one granting the benefit of lending.

And if the banker rendered other services to the depositor, apart from the inherent advantage to this type of loan that brings about so many benefits to him, he shall only be owed the corresponding stipend for them, unless, as is reasonable, he shall want to fulfill them gratuitously as compensation for the benefit of being chosen among all other bankers to carry out the deposit with him and give him access to so many advantages, or unless he renders these services as gifts to attract merchants and exchange dealers to enter the money in his bank. That is why in this matter I would not worry the merchants and exchange dealers, especially since if a banker were ungrateful and wanted stipends on top of the great advantages and profits gained from the deposits, he would deserve the withdrawal of these. And since the merchants and exchange dealers rightly believe these are gratuitous, if one of them did not want to carry it out gratuitously, there shall be many others willing to readily carry it out. That is why the merchants and exchange dealers who find out *a posteriori* that the services they thought were free of charge were not, are not forced to pay them. They did not intend to buy them but to receive them as compensation for the greater benefits they were conceding with their choice, and they would have easily found someone to give them free of charge. Because of this, if the banker intends to charge for the services, he shall have to say it beforehand so that the merchants and exchange dealers are bound to pay them. We shall later explain this more carefully when we deal with business management.

As for the second type of bankers, all the doctors agree that they can licitly receive a stipend from each one of the merchants who does business with their bank. Receiving, counting, and safekeeping the money; counting again when returning it; carrying a record of the transactions with third parties; giving them a copy, all with the risk of making mistakes in counting, examining, settling accounts; accepting bills of exchange from those who at that particular time do not have the money in the bank and being responsible for their debts—all of this has a price, so much the greater because in order to render these services, a person of a certain category and with some talent, ability, and qualifications is required, and so much greater the greater the profits they earn. The stipend is not appraised by law but is left to the parties' discretion. That is why the merchants in whose benefit the banker renders these services usually pay the banker at the end of the fairs what is proportionate to the managed business according to the prudent man's judgment.

It should be noted that although in some places they have the three types of persons we have talked about in the present argument, however, in others it is the merchants themselves who do the work of exchange dealers and call themselves bankers. What is more, in the same places where people who have posted a bond before the authorities in order to be depositaries and carry out the profession of bankers, there are, in addition to them, merchants who give money in exchange. And there are public bankers who practice trading with their own money and by their own authority grant exchanges with their own money to their own advantage or disadvantage.

Argument 409

On Some of the Ways in Which Money Is Paid for in the Exchanges

On Bills of Exchange

May the Bankers Licitly Receive Any Other Stipend?

In order to understand the practice of exchanging and in order to examine whether or not the bankers may licitly receive any other stipend, there are a few things worth noting. Many say the exchanges are received in many places, but Mercado states that neither in Rome nor in Seville do they commonly receive them.[1]

There are two ways in which bankers receive the money: (1) in cash, by giving currency to them; (2) by bills of exchange or any other letter of payment given to them, by virtue of which the person who has to pay the bill starts owing the bank the amount stipulated there to be paid into the account of the person who enters the bill in the bank.

Just as there are two ways of paying the money to the banker, there are also two ways in which he can pay: (1) in cash; (2) without utilizing currency. Without utilizing currency, payment can be made by transferring the amount to the bank account of one of the bank's debtors, from where it shall be charged; by

1. Tomás de Mercado, *Summa de tratos y contratos de mercaderes* (Seville, 1571), cap. 13.

furnishing a bill of exchange for a place where the creditor prefers; by setting up the bank as debtor for that sum in relation to the creditor who wishes the money to be paid into the account he has in the bank, or in relation to others to whom the creditor transfers the credit and they prefer to enter the amount into their bank account, or pay with it a debt that they have with the bank.

This is the reason why in the fair of Medina or in any other where many go to buy merchandise, even if there are many transactions carried out in cash, the majority are through documents that prove that the bank owes them or that it accepts paying by entering the money into the bank. This is how deals are closed—by compensating some debts with others and through the signature of bills of exchange issued to different places.

Also note that the bills of exchange are drafted utilizing several phrases, and so in some of them it says, "As soon as you receive or read the present document," or some such sentence. These payments are usually called "in full view," because the money has to be paid the moment the bill is shown and read. Other times it says, "On such day or in so many days, months, or whatever it is, after receiving the present document." In that case, the money must be paid on the appointed day. In some bills it says, "in such fair," for example, Medina or Amberes, "you shall pay a certain amount." In that case, one should abide by custom, and if custom were that such bills had to be paid at the beginning of the fairs, then they should be paid at that time. However, I believe the custom usually is to pay at the end of the fairs when there is a fixed time to pay off those debts, formalizing through signed documents the majority of the transactions previously carried out, since money is not so abundant that it allows buying with cash the enormous amount of merchandise that has been taken there for sale (if the payment is to be carried out in cash), and it does not allow the carrying out so many transactions. The merchants call this period in which accounts are closed and money is given to those who are creditors "setting up the tables" for the payments in the fair and "opening the exchanges."

What Soto says[2] on fairs and the practices of exchanges is in keeping with what has been said. His sources of information are the accounts of merchants. He says that in the kingdom of Castile there are four main fairs, spread out according to the four seasons of the year, and they correspond to another four fairs in Flanders and in other places. In these fairs they accept exchanges for other fairs held in different places, and for places where they do not have fairs. In a similar way, in other places and other fairs they accept exchanges for these fairs.

The first of these four fairs takes place in Medina del Campo in the month of May, and in them they set up the tables and open the exchanges on the fifteenth day of July, and the payments last until August 10. This fair corresponds to another one in Flanders in the month of September, where they set up the tables and open the exchanges on November 10, and the settlements last all month.

The second fair takes place in the other Medina, the one they call Rio Seco. There the exchanges open on September 15 and last until October 10. This fair corresponds to another in Flanders, which takes place at Christmas time. There they open the exchanges on February 10 and the settlements last until the end of the month.

The third fair takes place in Medina del Campo in October, and in it the exchanges open in December, and the settlements last until the end of the month. This fair corresponds to the fair of Resurrection in Flanders, where the exchanges open on May 10 and last all month.

The fourth fair takes places in the region of Villalón. Its exchanges open in the middle of Lent and last until Resurrection. It corresponds to the fair in Flanders in June, where the exchanges open in August and last until the end of the month.

---

2. Domingo de Soto, *De iustitia et iure, libri decem* (Salamanca, 1553), lib. 6, q. 12, art. 2.

However, sometimes the four fairs that take place in Spain, especially that of Medina del Campo, continue by order of the king until the arrival of the fleet from the New World, or for other reasons, according to Soto. The purpose of this practice of carrying out the exchanges between the Castilian fairs and those of Flanders is allowing only three months for the payment, which is the period of time until the next Flemish fair and is considered sufficient to send the bills of exchange from Castile. Inversely, the same amount of time is granted between the fairs of Flanders and those of Castile, because if in the fair that in May takes place in Medina an exchange dealer draws up the balance at the end of July or beginning of August for the fair of Flanders, the money should be paid in Flanders in the next fair, that is, the one in September, when the exchanges are opened there. According to Soto, the same happens regarding the other fairs that are related to each other.

The above should not be interpreted as if money in cash could not be taken for the exchanges at the beginning of the fair and during the year even if there were a need to do it; or as if the bills of exchange that have been sent in which a payment is ordered on a certain day, or as soon as they are handed over, cannot be paid at that moment and had to wait until the exchanges are open and the tables set up. Note that someone is not considered to be buying on credit if the price is debited from his own bank account, even if the payment is not in cash for the time being, because the banker shall pay in cash the balance due, in any case, at the end of the fair. In the fairs it is considered that someone is buying on credit when he buys to pay at some other time. Finally, you should know that the bills of exchange are not usually addressed to the banker, but to one of his representatives who will assume responsibility for the amounts indicated in the bills of exchange. The representative enters the money in his bank account so that the bank pays the money on the day specified in the bill of exchange—if its specifications were to pay an amount to whoever presents it—or receives the money on behalf of the one sending the bills of exchange if it is ordered in it that such amount of money be paid to its sender or representative in that place.

Once this is explained, Mercado, Soto, and Navarrus[3] report than in many places the custom is that the banker, when he pays the bills of exchange in cash, charges 5 or 6 per 1,000 over the amount paid, a commission he does not receive if the payment is not in cash but using bank accounts in any of the ways described above. Thus, when someone charges the bank what is owed to him, he receives the total amount of what the bill indicates, because when the banker enters the amount into the account he enters the total amount that he shall pay in cash when the time comes, unless there is a compensation that prevents him from paying in cash. However, and after all, if he pays the total in cash or pays part of the amount entered, the banker charges 5 or 6 per 1,000 of the amount he pays in cash. That is why the sellers of merchandise sell them more expensively to anyone paying through the bank. In addition to this, the seller shall have to wait until the end of the fair to collect. This explains why when selling in fairs, the merchants ask what the method of payment shall be before fixing a price.

In order to better understand when the things we are talking about take place, and in order to expose some abuses, we point out that when one deposits money in cash in the bank to withdraw it later, the banker does not charge this 5 or 6 per 1,000 but gives a free service. For the same reason, if the depositor sends bills of exchange or other similar ones, so that from his money something is given to another person, the banker does not receive anything for carrying out this delivery in cash since he does not have just motive to do so, nor do I think it is the custom. What is more, in some places the banker usually gives

3. Mercado, *Summa*, cap. 13; Soto, *De iustitia et iure*, lib. 6, q. 11; Martín de Azpilcueta, *Comentario resolutorio de usuras* (Salamanca, 1556), cap. últ., no. 37; Azpilcueta, *Manual de confesores y penitentes* (Salamanca, 1556), cap. 17, no. 293.

the depositor an interest of 4 or 5 per 1,000 as compensation for the profit earned from using the money deposited, and in other places the custom is that if the depositor has deposited, for example, 10,000 *ducats*, he obtains credit with the banker for another 5,000, so that if the depositor authorizes the bank to make payments of up to 15,000 *ducats*, the bank takes charge of them and compels him to pay them without getting any stipend for that greater credit and the obligations he takes on himself.

Although it seems Soto accepts this at the end of the last article,[4] both practices are usurious by nature if the banker carries them out by virtue of a pact and not out of generosity or gratitude, as it would mean a profit originated in a loan since, as we have proved before, this type of deposit is equivalent to a loan. Navarrus[5] and Mercado agree with us in the place cited above.

But if the banker were to do it out of generosity and gratitude, as a reward for the benefit received and with the intention of encouraging the depositor with this favor to continue his deposit, it shall not be usury nor sin, as long as scandal is avoided.

In the cited chapter,[6] Mercado says that this is so only when whoever sends the bill of exchange does not have any deposit in the bank where the payment is to be authorized, because, in that case, in order for the bank to feel compelled to pay that money at the end of the fair, it is an accepted custom in some places to charge 5 or 6 per 1,000 to be paid in cash in addition to the stipend usually charged for managing the business of its usual clients. He considers this is a good enough reason, because the guarantor may licitly charge an adequate price for the obligation he assumes in lending, as we saw in argument 319. So the same may be said of the banker who assumes the obligation of paying that money at the end of the fair in the name of whoever sends

4. Soto, *De iustitia et iure*, lib. 6, q. 11, art. últ., ad finem.

5. Azpilcueta, *Comentario*, cap. últ., no. 4; Azpilcueta, *Manual*, no. 293; Mercado, *Summa*, cap. 13.

6. Mercado, *Summa*, cap. 13.

the bill of exchange: he may justly receive a reward. Aside from this, Mercado points out that the bills of exchange are sent to the representative in the following way: In such a fair you shall pay 1,000 and shall consign this bill in the bank with a 6 per 1,000 commission for paying it. The point of this, he says, is that 1,006 are deposited in the bank so that whoever presents the bill can charge the total amount to the person who sold him the merchandise, and the bank pays him in this way at the end of the fair. When the banker pays in cash a part of the money at the end of the fair to the person who presented the bill or to whoever he ordered it be paid to, the banker shall receive the 6 per 1,000 of what he paid in cash. The result of which is, all things considered, that the 6 per 1,000 is paid by the person who sent the bill and in it he cedes that 6 per 1,000 to whoever accepted it as means of payment. The 6 per 1,000 shall go to the banker if he pays the bill in cash. And whoever draws the bill is acting in his own interest when he concedes that 6 per 1,000, because since he does not have money in the bank, he would have to take it in exchange in his own name, and exchanges are very expensive during the fair, as there are many who want them in order to be able to carry out their dealings. But once the fair is over they are not as expensive. Therefore, instead of taking money in exchange, they prefer to draw a bill with a 6 per 1,000 commission so that the banker takes responsibility for paying the 1,000 when the fair is over.

Soto[7] seems to be of this opinion, although he does not explain it as clearly and suggests that in the kingdom of Castile the law says that the 6 per 1,000 should be paid to the banker when the payment is settled in cash. But Navarrus is right when he rejects this opinion, because if a law existed before approved by Ferdinand and Isabella, they themselves revoked it.[8] Navarrus absolutely condemns the custom of charging 5 or 6 per 1,000

7. Soto, *De iustitia et iure*, lib. 6, q. 11, art. 1.

8. N. R. 5.18.5.

to the person to whom a payment is made by order of whoever deposited the money in the bank[9] and says that the banker has the obligation of restituting that 6 per 1,000 to the person it was charged to. The only exception is the case where the person that should receive the restitution has already sold the merchandise at a higher price for reason of such charge or when he simply wants to exonerate him. But in this matter mere presumption is not enough, and the reason for this is that everything the banker does he does as a service for the person who gives the order to pay that sum of money and in whose name he acts. Therefore, it is to him he should ask for the stipend and not to the person the banker pays.

Navarrus supposes that the custom is that, when the payment is in cash, they do not consign in the bank 1,000 and then 6 that the banker shall receive in the end, but only the 1,000 owed to the person for whom the money is consigned. He even says that it happened to him to go to the bank to collect some money they had sent him in a bill of exchange from another place, and the banker refused to pay him without charging the 6 per 1,000, and since all his arguments were useless to convince him, he was not able to rightly receive the money. I shall give my opinion on this matter in a few conclusions.

First conclusion: In the case where the banker takes responsibility for paying an amount of money at the end of the fair on behalf of someone who does not have money deposited in the bank, it does not seem that the banker should be condemned for collecting 6 per 1,000 of what he pays, especially if it is the custom there. This is because he has just reason to charge it, namely, accepting the obligation, as Soto and Mercado rightly say.

Second conclusion: That interest should be formally or virtually paid by the person in whose name the money was entered into the bank in the first place, and not by those who are to be paid. This may be proved with Navarrus's argument: that the obligation

9. Azpilcueta, *Comentario*, no. 37; Azpilcueta, *Manual*, cap. 17, no. 293.

the banker assumes, in truth, is assumed by himself and not by the person in whose name the money was first deposited and in whose favor he pledges to carry out the payments. Therefore, that is the person who should pay the stipend and not those to whom the payments are made. If, as Mercado says happens, someone who owes another person 1,000 *ducats* consigns 1,006 in the bank because of the stipend the banker shall receive at the end, it is he who shall formally pay such stipend. However, if he were only to consign 1,000 because that is the value of what he bought from the other person, and this person knew about or should know about the operation, the banker would be able to retain from those 1,000 the amount corresponding to his payment and, in such case, the person in whose favor the money was consigned in the bank shall pay the stipend.

Third conclusion: When 1,000 *ducats* are consigned in the bank and that is the amount that has to be paid in cash to the person in whose name they were consigned, without this person having any reason to think differently, the banker may charge for himself the stipend taking it from the 1,000 *ducats* he pays in cash, as one should deem that he wanted to obligate himself with the requirement of receiving the usual stipend. It is evident that the person to whom the 1,000 were owed in their entirety has a right to request from the person who consigned the money to pay the 1,000 *ducats*.

Fourth conclusion: When there has not been a previous commitment on the banker's part to pay in cash in someone else's name, the banker may not deduct any amount from what he pays in cash, but must make do with the stipend that in any case he should collect from the person whose business he manages. This may be proved because the counting and paying of that money, if he gives it so that it is returned to him in the same place, has the characteristics of a loan, because of which he may not licitly receive more than what was loaned.

Here, I must refer to another abuse bankers usually put into practice. When there is an amount of money consigned in their bank to pay at the end of the fair, if the person for whom it was consigned in the first place in order to pay creditors from whom he has bought merchandise demands that the money be paid before the end of the fair, the bankers usually give it to him but charging the interest, which is usually charged on money given in exchange to other places or any other interest. Therefore, whatever is received in this way is usurious and must be restituted, as the anticipated payment is virtually a loan, because of which anything that is received for it shall be usury, unless it is received for reason of the profit ceasing that the banker incurs when he anticipates the payment, which rarely happens. So much more shall it be considered sinful, when the time of payment comes and in order to prevent the payment from being delayed, to receive something from the creditor. So, too, do these have obligation to restitute, because everything received in this way is only halfway voluntary and is received unjustly when it is not a sign of the generous spirit of the giver.

Argument 410

On Exchanges and the Different Value of Money in Different Places, Not in Comparison to Small Coins Any Longer but Because of Concurrent Circumstances

Thus, We End Our Study on Money

In argument 406 we introduced a distinction in the value of money, considering it according to a double aspect. In the second of these, all money—not this or that from a certain region—is worth more in one place than in another comparing equal amounts in one and the other, even if in one and the other place they are equal coins as far as material, weight, metal alloy, and the seal itself, and to which the law has assigned the same value in comparison to the other coins in the place. We were saying this value does not originate in the currency itself, but in the circumstances and is a very inconstant value that is not fixed in an indivisible point but moves within certain limits. It is like the value of the other merchandise, which as long as it is not appraised by the law is not fixed in one exact point. What we are trying to find out now is whether for reason of the difference in this type of value it is licit to increase the price of exchanges from one place to another or whether it is more convenient to reduce it sometimes according to the greater or lesser value that money has in that place.

Soto, Navarrus, and others respond affirmatively,[1] and their opinion may be proven because the commutation of two things that are equal in value is in itself licit. Therefore, if at one point 360 *maravedis* in Flanders are worth the same as 400 in Medina (for the scarcity of coin in Flanders and the abundance in Medina, and for other concurrent reasons), it shall be licit—if all other circumstances are equal—to exchange 360 *maravedis* given in Flanders for 400 to be delivered in Medina. And, conversely, it shall be licit to exchange 400 given in Medina for 360 to be delivered in Flanders, the same as it is licit to exchange 100 units of wine or oil given in the Spanish territories for 80 that are given in Flanders. And, conversely, 80 that are given in Flanders shall be exchanged for 100 to be given in the Spanish territories, as 80 units of wine or oil are worth in Flanders the same as 100 in the Spanish territories, for which reason wine and oil are taken to Flanders.

For this reason, it is frequently licit to exchange a greater amount of currency, which is handed over in the place where the currency is worth less, for a lesser quantity that shall be handed over where as currency it is worth more. And, conversely, it is also licit to exchange a lesser amount of currency where as such currency it is worth more for a greater quantity to hand over where as currency it is worth less. According to Soto, in the place cited, and Mercado,[2] the exchange dealers take into account today this greater or lesser value of money for their exchanges from one place to another. And this is the way they justify the exchanges they carry out.

1. Domingo de Soto, *De iustitia et iure, libri decem* (Salamanca, 1553), lib. 6, q. 12, art. 2ff.; Martín de Azpilcueta, *Comentario resolutorio de usuras* (Salamanca, 1556), cap. últ., nos. 51, 59, 65ff.; Azpilcueta, *Manual de confesores y penitentes* (Salamanca, 1556), cap. 17, no. 294ff.

2. Soto, *De iustitia et iure*, lib. 6, q. 12, art. 2ff.; Tomás de Mercado, *Summa de tratos y contratos de mercaderes* (Seville, 1571), lib. De los cambios, caps. 5ff.

Against this argument, which is the most important foundation for the exchanges from one place to another as they are practiced today, someone could argue that if in the place where there is less money and more need of it, it is licit to exchange a lesser amount in order to give back a greater amount where there is a greater abundance and lesser need of it—and this because of the circumstances, money is worth less in one place than in another—then it follows that it is licit in one and the same place to exchange a smaller amount of money, at the time when in that place it is scarce and there is a greater need of it, for another greater amount to be given back at a time of greater abundance of money and lesser need. Now then, no one shall admit the consequent and, in consequence, neither the antecedent.

Soto, in the cited article 2, denies that one thing follows the other and gives no other reason but that when money is given back in the same place and at a different time it will be a loan, and for reason of the loan nothing may be collected. But when the money is given back somewhere else there is an exchange of two things of equal value, although unequal in amount, which is licit.

However, this solution is not acceptable, because also in the loan, if what is given back is equal—at the time in which it is given back—to the value of what was loaned—at the time in which it was loaned—the contract shall be licit, without there being any problem in giving back a greater amount than what was received. For example, it shall be licit to loan 2 units of wheat at the time when each one is worth 2 *ducats* in order to get back 4 units at the time of harvest when it is estimated that each unit shall be worth 1 *ducat*, since here is seen the equality between what is given and what is received, even if there is inequality in the amount or number of units. What is more, it would be usury to lend 4 units of wheat in times in which each one is worth a *ducat* to be given back as many units when it is estimated that each shall be worth 2 *ducats*. So it was said in that place in the ruling

Naviganti de usuris,[3] and Soto himself approves of this, because of which, if a lesser amount of money, because of its scarcity and need, is now worth the same as a greater amount will be worth later in that same place for the abundance they expect, there is no reason to deny that one thing follows the other.

The true reason why this inference should be denied appeared at the end of argument 406: Money, regardless of whether there is scarcity and need or abundance, should never be considered merchandise in relation to the place where it is, but always retains the price or value appraised by law or accepted by custom (I am talking about the countries in which the prices of coins are fixed and do not depend on the will or pact between the private persons), and, because of this, in relation to that place it is not worth more at one time than another. Its value varies only when exchanging for coins from another country, as was explained. One should take into account, however, that for reason of profit ceasing, because money was lent at a time in which there was less abundance of it in order to get it back when there was a greater one, one may receive an increase equivalent to the estimated profit ceasing. For example, at a time when money is scarce and therefore the price of things drops, if the person who has money had been thinking about buying things to make a profit or to support his family and had to do without this opportunity in order to lend money to someone else, then when giving the loan he may agree to an increment on the loaned capital that is equivalent to the estimated profit ceasing. Likewise, the one who when lending foresees that later he will have to buy at a higher price whatever he needs for his family, may agree to an increment equivalent to that loss occurring. In a similar way, if he was thinking of giving money in exchange for another place with a good profit, which he has to do without when accepting that the money be given back in the same place, he may agree to an increment equivalent to the profit he is being deprived of.

3. Ed. note: D. 5.19.19.

To sum up the whole matter of exchanges practiced from one place to another and to bring the rest of the argument to an end, we must consider simultaneously three rulings to judge whether the exchange is just or not, and to judge what increment it is just to collect in each case, and when—in order for the exchange to be just—not to collect any increment to begin with or even to receive a sum that is inferior to the one handed out. And we are not referring here to dry exchange, which we said enough of in argument 404, but to the rest of exchanges carried out from one place to another. We shall proceed with those three rulings but not in the same order in which they were presented.

The first ruling is the different value a coin may have in comparison to the petty coins. Thus, if the exchange is carried out reckoning in larger coins, such as *ducats*, *escudos*, or silver *reales* (which is the custom), and if the value of these coins is different in the place where the exchange is being carried out and in the place for which it is given, it has already been proven in argument 407 (against what some doctors think) that although one should consider somewhat this greater or lesser value, this should have a very small influence in the increase of the type of exchange, if it is to be considered just.

On the contrary, if the exchange is carried out expressing the amounts in petty coins (which is not frequently done), for example in *maravedis* to be given back in *reais* in Portugal, and vice versa, then, as the *maravedis* are worth in Castile more than the *reais* in Portugal, as was proven in that argument, one should take into consideration such difference of value. This is because, abstaining from other arguments that allow the type of exchange to rise or fall, if for 374 *reais* given in Portugal an equal amount of *maravedis* were received in Castile, it would not be an exchange of equal for equal and, thus, it would be unjust and there would be obligation to restitute, because in Portugal for those *reais* they would give us a little over 9 silver *reales* and, in Castile, for the *maravedis* they would give us 11 whole silver *reales*.

The second ruling is that of the formal or virtual transport of money from the place where the exchange dealer gives the money to the place where he receives it. By this ruling the exchange dealer may increase the exchange as much as the value of said transport is estimated according to the prudent people's judgment, taking into account the distance between both places, the difficulty of transport and all other circumstances, as we explained in argument 403 and the two following ones.

The third ruling is the different value of money in diverse places due to the abundance or scarcity of it, the need for it, and other circumstances, as we have explained in the present argument and in argument 406. But although by virtue of this ruling—and the same goes for the virtual transport—it is licit to frequently increase the exchange, it happens sometimes that by reason of this ruling it shall be necessary to reduce it so that the exchange is equitable and just, as, for example, when the value of the money in the place in which it is given is lower in comparison to its value in the place in which it has to be received, as has already been said. And if the value of the money in the place in which it is given is inferior in an equivalent amount to the cost of transport, then, in order for the contract to be equitable and just, the exchange should be carried out for equal sums of money, compensating the cost of transport with the inferior value of money in the place where it is given. If the cost of transport were to exceed that difference, the excess may be reflected in an increment in the amount to be received for the exchange. On the contrary, if the difference exceeds the cost of transport then and only then shall it be necessary to increase the amount of money given in comparison to the one received in order for the contract to be just.

However, neither the cost of transport nor the excess of value that money has for this third ruling can be fixed with all precision but shall be just within certain limits. That is why it is sufficient that the contracting parties do not break away from the limits of what is just. Consequently, the bounds specifying what is just in the exchanges, taking into account all the rulings for which the type of exchange may be increased or decreased, may not be fixed with all precision, and there shall be a greater laxness the more rulings there are according to which the justice of the exchange from one place to another is to be judged.

Soto says that when this third ruling may be applied, namely, charging an increment because money is worth more where the exchange dealer hands it over than where he receives it, it is not licit to charge on top of this another increment for reason of the virtual transport of the money, unless perhaps a very small quantity.[4] This may be confirmed because when you transport for me an amount of money from a place where it is worth less to another where it is worth more, the increase in value should be in my favor, as I pay for the transport. Therefore, if the exchange dealer charges a price for the formal or virtual transport, he may not licitly charge more because of the greater value money has there and, if he charges for reason of the greater value of money in that place, he may not charge for the transport, as he is not transporting anything for the person who takes the money in exchange.

Despite this argument, I believe it more plausible to state that it is licit to charge something for the virtual transport or, rather, for the discharge it means for the one asking for the exchange of not having to transport the money. This is evident because when giving the equivalent value to him in the place where he needs the money he is really discharged of the job of transporting and taking it there, and that is something that deserves remuneration and may be sold. Therefore, in order to accomplish this in his favor I may receive a just stipend, notwithstanding the fact that I may *per accidens* get the job done easily and without expense through a correspondent I have there, as was explained in argument 403. This is so because to the prudent merchants' judgment, 370 in Flanders are worth the same as 400 in Medina,

4. Soto, *De iustitia et iure*, lib. 6, q. 12, art. 2.

for example, and apart from that, the virtual transport of money from Flanders to Medina (or rather being discharged of the need of taking care of the transport) is worth another 10. Therefore, the exchange is licit when the exchange dealer gives 400 in Medina for 370 that shall be given back in Flanders, so that 360 are given as equal value to the money he received in Medina, and the other 10 for saving the transport from Flanders to Medina. For the same reason, if the exchange dealer gives 360 in Flanders he may receive in Medina something more than 400, so that 400 are the payment for the equal value of money given in Flanders, and the excess is given for having discharged from the need of transporting the money.

The conclusion is obvious, as in neither of the two cases is there a formal transport of the money but simply an avoiding of the annoyance of transporting it and, in both cases, leaving aside the amount received for this, there is an equality between what is given and what is received if one takes into account the difference in value of the money in one place and the other. Soto would not deny the antecedent as in such exchange nothing is received for reason of the greater value of the money in the place in which the exchange dealer gives it, as the money is worth less in Medina, where he gives it, than in Flanders, and that is why in Flanders less money is received than what is given in Medina. And Soto himself states that when an increment is not received for reason of the greater value that money has in that place, it may be received for reason of virtual transport. And notice that the exchange dealer, apart from what he receives for reason of the virtual transport, does not receive an increment either in the amount of money or in its value where the money is worth more. Rather, where it is worth less he receives an increment, not in the value but in the amount of money in order to compensate the greater value that his money has in the other place.

To the argument we have presented in favor of the contrary opinion we must say: In the first place, it implies something that is false, namely, that the exchange dealer receives the money in the place where the money is worth more. Let us add that the opposite is true when the money is really carried, but not when the equivalent is given in a place for the equivalent in another and the one who receives it saves himself the job of transporting it, because then what each one gives is valuable for him in the place where he gives it and not in any other place. Also, the person who is requested by another to discharge him through that commutation of the annoyance of transporting the money may receive a just stipend for his involvement.

From what we have just said it is evident that one should not condemn the fact that an exchange dealer who gives 360 in Flanders receives in Medina more than what he himself gives in Medina for the 360 they give him back in Flanders, because Soto says that when there was no difference in the value of money in two places, it was a practice in his time that an exchange dealer gave in Medina 410 in exchange for receiving 360 in Flanders and, on the contrary, when he gave exchange in Flanders for Medina, for the 360 he gave in Flanders he received 430 in Medina. However, Soto condemns this last case, as he says that if the first exchange was equitable, the second was not so.

In spite of this, both exchanges are just for the following reason: 360 in Flanders may be worth, because of the state of affairs, the same as 420 in Medina, and so, if an exchange is solicited in Medina for Flanders, the exchange dealer acts justly when subtracting 10 from the 420 for the job of discharging the person who asks for the exchange. And if an exchange is solicited from Flanders to Medina, he justly adds 10 to the 420, which they are to give him back in Medina for his work in discharging the person who asks for the exchange.

As said above, the just value of money in the different places and in a certain moment in time cannot be determined with all precision but fluctuates between certain limits the same as the rest of merchandise that is not appraised by law and, since the just price of the virtual transport of money from one place to another cannot be determined with all precision either, it follows that the just price of the exchanges, not only in different places but in one and the same place and at one and the same moment in time, is situated within a range of a certain amplitude. Moreover, the circumstances that make the value of money and its transport increase or decrease change easily, all of which makes it logical for the just price of exchanges to change and be different, not only regarding exchanges between different places, but also regarding exchanges in one and the same place at different times, mainly, because when the amount of money increases or decreases, the just prices of the rest of things vary, as do the just profits pursued with the exchanges, since men do not want to employ their money for exchanges unless these bring about greater benefits; otherwise, they prefer using it in other endeavors.

I would like to caution here that we do not mean that the examples presented here dealing with exchanges carried out between one place and another, and which may be found in the doctors' writings, reflect real life, as if the practice of exchanges should adjust itself to them, seeing that with the passing of time circumstances vary and we find very different practices.

Because the natural just price of all things depends on the common estimation in one place (as said in argument 348 and frequently in others), we should not consider the commonly accepted price for exchanges from one place to another unjust, but rather just and a standard to judge whether the exchanges that greatly move away from it because of excess or insufficiency, exceed what is just. This must be understood as long as the actual price has not been manipulated by means of monopoly or other frauds. For if those who have the money agree that neither one of them shall give in exchange except with an agreed upon increment, and that increment exceeds the price that would be current if it were not for the monopoly, those who provoked that excessive and unjust price, certainly, do not only mortally sin but are forced to restitute that increment to those who paid it.

Likewise, if before the fair takes place, or at the very beginning of it, some take all the money there is in that place to exchange in different places in order to give it later during the fair with a much greater increment and at their own discretion to those who would need it, since they are the only ones who have money, they certainly also mortally sin and are forced to restitute if they give it for a price that exceeds the strictly just one that would be current if it were not for them and is the equitable price.

For if neither these nor the others exceeded the strictly just price, I would not force them to restitute, according to what we said on this matter in argument 345, and was later proven. There may be, certainly, a sin against charity against one's own brother and against the country, a sin that deserves being prohibited and punished, as was said before. But if any, foreseeing that the money shall be very expensive in one fair, took before this fair exchanges for diverse places for the amount of all the money that there is in that place in order to give exchanges later at the maximum just price that is equitable given the circumstances, he should not be condemned of mortal sin, because in acting as he did he has used his right and has harmed no one. His actions are born of his ability and experience in doing business. This principle must be accepted as long as that usual price does not obey any ruling for which something may be obtained unjustly, as would be if for an extension in time a greater price were usually given for the money offered for exchange: that would be a sin with obligation to restitute the excessive increment, even if it is a usually accepted practice. As Navarrus well notes,[5] the abundance of buyers, when the thing is sold unjustly, does not make the price of the thing increase. Therefore, the just price of the thing is not reflected in the common use.

5. Azpilcueta, *Comentario*, cap. últ., no. 59.

Finally, we must observe two things: first, in the exchanges sometimes the name of *ducat* is understood as having one and the same value in the place where the exchange is given and in the place where it is later paid. So the increases or deductions are expressed adding or taking away *ducats* from the sum to be paid in the place for which the exchange is given. For example, in a certain place 110 or 115 *ducats* are received for which bills of exchange are given so that in another place 100 *ducats* are paid. This means that an increment of 10 or 15 *ducats* are received. I understand this to be so even when the *ducats* have a different value appraised by law or accepted by custom in the different provinces. It happens in Portugal, where the *ducat* is worth 400 *reais*, but only 10 silver *reales*, while in Castile it is worth 375 *maravedis* or also 11 silver *reales* and 1 *maravedi*. That is why, when exchanges are carried out from Castile to Portugal, expressing the sums of money in terms of *ducats*, we may apply what we have described above. As the Castilian *ducat* is worth 1 silver *real* more than the one in Portugal, if the exchange is given from Castile to Portugal with an increase of 3 or 4 percent, 100 *ducats* are received, for example, in Castile and letters of payment are given in Portugal for 113 or 114 *ducats*. Since 100 *ducats* in Castile and 110 in Portugal are equal quantities (as both quantities are worth 1,100 silver *reales*), the person who gives said exchange from Castile to Portugal receives an increment of 3 or 4 Portuguese *ducats*. And if with the same increment an exchange were given from Portugal to Castile, 100 *ducats* would be received in Portugal and bills of exchange would be given for Castile for a value of a little over 93½ or 94½.

Because in Flanders there were frequent variations in the value of coins, in 1527 the merchants adopted by common agreement a fixed value for those coins, which had to be maintained among them forever, even if their value changed in one region or another. And so, in the bills of exchange that were given in Flanders, they often said, "You shall pay so many *ducats*," the third part, for example, in gold, and the rest in silver according to the valuation of coins in 1527.

Sometimes, however, the merchants do not use in their contracts the term *ducat* with the valuation this coin has in the place from which or for which the exchange is given, but with a conventional valuation that they themselves establish when the contract of exchange is drafted, namely, increasing or reducing the value of the *ducat* in the place in which the exchange is to be paid, according to the circumstances. This is the way that 100 *ducats* worth 360 *maravedis* were usually received in Flanders in exchange for another 100 worth 400 *maravedis* to be paid in Medina. And in Medina bills of exchange were given in the following way: You shall pay 100 *ducats* worth 400 *maravedis* each. And since neither then nor now did they have in Medina *ducats* with such value, the merchants gave them an imaginary reality for their exchanges and businesses. In a similar way today do they "create" *ducats* and *escudos* for different places with different values, according to what the merchants agree among themselves. Navarrus[6] was strongly against these imaginary *ducats* but then changed his mind[7] and believed they should be admitted.

The second thing that must be observed is that what has been said on this matter of exchanges should be interpreted with benevolence, because we have stretched the doctrine to the limit of what is just in order that it may be used as a guideline to confessors and others who must respond to questions on the subject, so that they do not force the exchangers to restitute when they do not have obligation to do so and do not condemn what does not deserve to be condemned. But that does not mean that very frequently one should not advise men to abstain from such exchanges because of the abuses that in them they frequently commit and for the danger of losing the eternal salvation to

---

6. Azpilcueta, *Comentario*, cap. últ., no. 53.
7. Azpilcueta, *Manual*, cap. 17, no. 302.

which the not-too-God-fearing who devote themselves to this business expose themselves.

As far as whether the intermediaries employed by the exchange dealers and all the others who help in illicit exchanges sin and are forced to restitute, what was said in argument 331 about those who cooperate with usury can also be applied to them.

About the Contributors

Jordan J. Ballor (Dr. theol., University of Zurich) is a research fellow at the Acton Institute for the Study of Religion & Liberty and serves as executive editor of the *Journal of Markets & Morality*. He is also the author of *Covenant, Causality, and Law: A Study in the Theology of Wolfgang Musculus* (Vandenhoeck & Ruprecht, 2012) and *Ecumenical Babel: Confusing Economic Ideology and the Church's Social Witness* (Christian's Library Press, 2010).

Jeannine Emery has a degree in Spanish Literature and a master's in nonfiction writing. She works as an editor and translator in both English and Spanish. She lives in Buenos Aires, Argentina.

Stephen J. Grabill (PhD, Calvin Theological Seminary) serves as senior research scholar in theology and director of programs at the Acton Institute for the Study of Religion & Liberty. He is editor emeritus of the *Journal of Markets & Morality*, as well as author of *Rediscovering the Natural Law in Reformed Theological Ethics* (Eerdmans, 2006) and editor of *Sourcebook in Late-Scholastic Monetary Theory* (Lexington, 2007).

Rudolf Schuessler (Dr. rer. pol., LMU Munich) is professor of philosophy at the University of Bayreuth, Germany. He works on modern and scholastic practical ethics, and particularly on probabilism, just war theories, and economic thought. His publications include *Moral im Zweifel*, 2 vols. (Mentis, 2003 and 2006); "The Economic Thought of Luis de Molina," in *A Companion to Luis de Molina*, ed. Matthias Kaufmann and Alexander Aichele (Brill, 2014), 257–88; "Practical Ethics," in *The Cambridge History of Medieval Philosophy*, vol. 1, ed. Robert Pasnau (Cambridge University Press, 2014), 517–35; and "Business Morality at the Dawn of Modernity—the Cases of Angelo Corbinelli and Cosimo de' Medici," in *Between Creativity and Norm-Making*, ed. Sigrid Müller and Cornelia Schweiger (Brill, 2012), 131–48.

Christian's LIBRARY PRESS

Founded in 1979 by Gerard Berghoef and Lester DeKoster, **CHRISTIAN'S LIBRARY PRESS** has been committed to publishing influential texts on church leadership, the vocation of work, and stewardship for more than thirty years. During that time Berghoef and DeKoster wrote significant works including *The Deacons Handbook*, *The Elders Handbook*, and *God's Yardstick*, which still are in demand today. After the passing of Lester DeKoster in 2009, the imprint is now administered by the Acton Institute for the Study of Religion & Liberty. For more information about Christian's Library Press, visit www.clpress.com.

ACTON INSTITUTE

With its commitment to pursue a society that is free and virtuous, the **ACTON INSTITUTE FOR THE STUDY OF RELIGION & LIBERTY** is a leading voice in the international environmental and social policy debate. With offices in Grand Rapids, Michigan, and Rome, Italy, as well as affiliates in four other nations around the world, the Acton Institute is uniquely positioned to comment on the sound economic and moral foundations necessary to sustain humane environmental and social policies. The Acton Institute is a nonprofit, ecumenical think tank working internationally to "promote a free and virtuous society characterized by individual liberty and sustained by religious principles." For more on the Acton Institute, please visit www.acton.org.

Sources in Early Modern Economics, Ethics, and Law

Jordan J. Ballor and Stephen J. Grabill, General Editors

Books in This Series

A Treatise on the Alteration of Money
Juan de Mariana
Translated by Patrick T. Brannan • Annotations by Stephen J. Grabill
Introduction by Alejandro A. Chafuen

On the Law in General
Girolamo Zanchi
Translated by Jeffrey J. Veenstra • Introduction by Stephen J. Grabill

On Law and Power
Johannes Althusius
Translated by Jeffrey J. Veenstra • Introductions by Stephen J. Grabill and John Witte Jr.

On Exchange and Usury
Thomas Cajetan
Translated by Patrick T. Brannan • Introduction by Raymond de Roover

On Righteousness, Oaths, and Usury
Wolfgang Musculus
Translated by Todd M. Rester • Introduction by Jordan J. Ballor

On Exchange
Martín de Azpilcueta
Translated by Jeannine Emery • Introduction by Rodrigo Muñoz

A T[illegible]oney
Luis de Molina
Translated by Jeannine Emery • Introduction by Rudolf Schuessler

The Mosaic Polity
Franciscus Junius
Translated by Todd M. Rester • Edited by Andrew M. McGinnis

Of the Law of Nature
Matthew Hale
Edited by David S. Sytsma

On Sale, Securities, and Insurance
Leonardus Lessius
Translated by Wim Decock and Nicholas De Sutter • Introduction by Wim Decock

Made in the USA
Las Vegas, NV

47463469R00105